# JUMPSTART!

M000220894

*Jumpstart! Creativity* contains over 70 games and activities that any primary teacher can use to quickly and easily boost students' creative and critical thinking skills, allowing their thinking to flourish. Now in its second edition, the book contains fresh material that will help children to engage with the new National Curriculum.

Applicable across a wide age and ability range, *Jumpstart! Creativity* is designed to help children learn to generate, organise and refine their own ideas and to explore, question and connect knowledge presented to them in the classroom. Focussing on getting the children to do the thinking work, the jumpstarts cover:

- Creative thinking
- Creative questioning
- Creating reasoning
- Creative problem solving
- Creative wordplay

Filled with practical, fun-packed and easy-to-do activities, *Jumpstart! Creativity* is an essential companion to any primary teacher looking to inspire creativity and independent thinking in their students.

**Steve Bowkett** is a former teacher and author of numerous books for teachers. He visits schools to run creative writing workshops for children and works as an educational consultant specialising in the areas of thinking skills and problem solving, creativity and literacy.

# Jumpstart!

For a full list of titles in this series visit
www.routledge.com/Jumpstart/book-series/JUMP

## Jumpstart! Geography
Engaging activities for
ages 7-12
*Sarah Whitehouse and Mark Jones*

## Jumpstart! Thinking Skills and Problem Solving
Games and activities for
ages 7-14
*Steve Bowkett*

## Jumpstart! Maths (2nd Edition)
Maths activities and games for
ages 5-14
*John Taylor*

## Jumpstart! Spanish and Italian
Engaging activities for
ages 7–12
*Catherine Watts and
Hilary Phillips*

## Jumpstart! French and German
Engaging activities for
ages 7–12
*Catherine Watts and
Hilary Phillips*

## Jumpstart! Drama
Games and activities for
ages 5–11
*Teresa Cremin, Roger McDonald,
Emma Goff and Louise Blakemore*

## Jumpstart! Science
Games and activities for
ages 5–11
*Rosemary Feasey*

## Jumpstart! Storymaking
Games and activities for
ages 7–12
*Pie Corbett*

## Jumpstart! Poetry
Games and activities for
ages 7–12
*Pie Corbett*

## Jumpstart! Creativity
Games and activities for
ages 7–14
*Steve Bowkett*

## Jumpstart! ICT
ICT activities and games for ages
7–14
*John Taylor*

## Jumpstart! Numeracy
Maths activities and games for
ages 5–14
*John Taylor*

## Jumpstart! Literacy
Key Stage 2/3 literacy games
*Pie Corbett*

# JUMPSTART!
# CREATIVITY

## GAMES AND ACTIVITIES FOR
## AGES 7–14

Second edition

**Steve Bowkett**

Routledge
Taylor & Francis Group

LONDON AND NEW YORK

Second edition published 2018
by Routledge
2 Park Square, Milton Park, Abingdon, Oxon OX14 4RN

and by Routledge
711 Third Avenue, New York, NY 10017

*Routledge is an imprint of the Taylor & Francis Group, an informa business*

© 2018 Steve Bowkett

The right of Steve Bowkett to be identified as author of this work has been asserted by him in accordance with sections 77 and 78 of the Copyright, Designs and Patents Act 1988.

All rights reserved. No part of this book may be reprinted or reproduced or utilised in any form or by any electronic, mechanical, or other means, now known or hereafter invented, including photocopying and recording, or in any information storage or retrieval system, without permission in writing from the publishers.

*Trademark notice*: Product or corporate names may be trademarks or registered trademarks, and are used only for identification and explanation without intent to infringe.

First edition published by Routledge 2008.

*British Library Cataloguing in Publication Data*
A catalogue record for this book is available from the British Library

*Library of Congress Cataloging in Publication Data*
Names: Bowkett, Stephen, author.
Title: Jumpstart! creativity : games & activities for ages 7-14 / Steve Bowkett.
Description: Milton Park, Abingdon, Oxon ; New York, NY : Routledge, 2018.
Identifiers: LCCN 2017053501| ISBN 9780815367956 (hardback) | ISBN 9780815367963 (pbk.) | ISBN 9781351256155 (ebook)
Subjects: LCSH: Education, Elementary—Activity programs. | Educational games.
Classification: LCC LB1592 .B69 2018 | DDC 371.33/7—dc23
LC record available at https://lccn.loc.gov/2017053501

ISBN: 978-0-8153-6795-6 (hbk)
ISBN: 978-0-8153-6796-3 (pbk)
ISBN: 978-1-351-25616-2 (ebk)

Typeset in Palatina and Scala Sans
by Swales & Willis Ltd, Exeter, Devon, UK

# Contents

Acknowledgements                                    viii
Introduction                                          ix

1   Jumpstart creative thinking                        1

The pyramid of creativity                              1
Alpha stones                                           5
Footprints                                             8
CSI – Crime Scene Investigation                        9
The detective game                                    10
Theme collage                                         15
The inkblot game                                      16
What could it be?                                     18
Heath Robinson machines                               18
Concept flags                                         19
The criss-cross game                                  21
Problem solver grid                                   23
Big it up, shrink it down                             29
Odd-one-out-and-in                                    30
Sensory journey                                       34
Sensory journey card game                             38
Sound FX                                              38
What colour is this music?                            40
Perceptual filtering                                  42

2   Jumpstart creative questioning                    45

Open or closed?                                       46
'Answer questions' or 'question questions'?           46
A question a day                                      48

Twenty questions                                    49
Question hooks                                      51
Question star                                       52
Question web                                        55
A matter of fact                                    57
A medley of question games                          58
Question quotes                                     59

3   Jumpstart creative reasoning                     60

Creative cut ups                                    60
Prediction strips                                   63
Structure and function                              67
Artist and instructor                               71
The 'if . . . then . . .' game                      72
The 'because' game                                  73
Narrative lines                                     76
3D diamond ranking                                  79
Ideas matrix                                        80
Emotions graph                                      81
The NOW spider                                      84
3D flowchart                                        85
Matchbox mysteries                                  86

4   Jumpstart creative problem solving               89

Ways of doing – strategic thinking                  90
The luckily/unluckily game                          92
'What if . . . ?' circle                            94
Letters to the editor                               95
Viewpoints                                          95
Decision alley                                      97
Finding the balance                                 97
'Smilemmas'                                         98
Iceberg thinking                                   100
The dilemmas game                                  102

| | | |
|---|---|---|
| 5 | Jumpstart creative wordplay | 104 |
| | 'This product comes with a lifetime guarantee' – Looking at language | 105 |
| | Adjectival names | 106 |
| | A medley of word games | 108 |
| | Connective chains | 114 |
| | A melange of motifs | 115 |
| | Urban legends | 120 |
| | Random poem | 122 |
| | Word pyramid | 126 |
| | Spot the difference | 129 |
| | Semiopathy | 129 |
| | Jokes | 130 |
| | Playing with proverbs | 133 |
| | New words and word combos | 135 |
| | Making new metaphors | 137 |
| | The flinty wind – multisensory metaphors | 139 |
| | The acronym game | 141 |
| | Wordplay card games | 141 |
| | Synonym/antonym tree | 143 |
| | Satnav | 144 |
| | Choose your own adventure | 145 |

# Acknowledgements

Grateful thanks to my friend Tony Hitchman for once again lending his artistic talents to one of my ventures. My appreciation also to Imporient for allowing me to mention their company name.

# Introduction

## WHY IS CREATIVITY USEFUL?

Interest in a creative approach to teaching and learning is more widespread now than it has been for many years. This is I suspect partly a backlash against the very prescriptive content-led curriculum that teachers and children have had to endure for so long. Many teachers I meet feel strongly that the educational regime of levels, targets and objectives driven as it is by batteries of assessments, tests and league tables has become too mechanical, overly pressured and emotionally sterile. As one head teacher said to me recently, 'Sometimes I feel that the human heart of education has disappeared from the classroom'.

My own opinion, backed by thirty years' experience of working in schools, is that a more creative approach to teaching and learning can help to redress the balance. And it is an approach that I aim to explore with you, exemplified by plenty of games, activities and techniques that I hope you will find to be useful and practical across the curriculum. Creativity in the classroom should never be regarded as a mere 'add on', something that we as teachers are expected to do as well as all our other tasks. Creativity puts the emphasis on children doing more thinking for themselves about the knowledge we offer them. It is about children generating ideas, organising information, reflecting upon and questioning concepts. It is, if you like, an attitude that we cultivate in our children to help them make more sense of the world they live in. The fundamental goal of that attitude is for our children (and us as their teachers) to be *unafraid of ideas*. As Jacob Bronowski said, 'We are not here to worship what is known, but to question it'. That fearlessness in exploring ideas turns knowledge and information into understanding, which is I think what being educated means.

## CREATIVE PRINCIPLES

The creative classroom obviously includes both teachers and children. The games in this book show children how to develop their own thinking and creative skills. As teachers we can maximise the effect of these activities by establishing the right environment through observing certain general principles.

- The principle of valuing. Nothing inhibits creative thinking more than the fear of getting an answer wrong. When we ask children to think, we must value the outcomes of that thinking. The thinking itself might be shaky, ideas may be illogical, conclusions might be erroneous – but that's part of the learning process. Whatever the outcome, we can sincerely praise the mental effort that went into the task.
- The principle of flexibility within a structure. If we make tasks too prescriptive, we limit children's thinking. If we make tasks too vague, then the children can flounder, not knowing what to think or how to think effectively. When we equip children with a range of strategies for thinking and structure tasks so that they can use those strategies to have ideas of their own, their creativity will flourish.
- The principle of patience. As teachers perhaps we are too often tempted simply to tell children the right answers or to do their thinking for them. Learning to think powerfully, and thinking itself, take time. Of course we are under pressure to 'deliver the curriculum', but if we ask our children to think, then we must create the opportunity for them to do just that. However, as the children's abilities develop they will be able to think more quickly and in more sophisticated ways. Your patience early on will bring benefits later.
- The principle of 'going beyond the given'. As you dip into this book you will see that the way I have described some activities slants them towards English, or more towards Geography or Biology or Technology, etc. Apply the same creative skills you're teaching the children – go beyond the given and see how any given activity can have other applications. The most powerful way to develop children's creativity is to demonstrate the creative attitude yourself.

## THE ORGANISATION OF THE BOOK

The activities in *Jumpstart! Creativity* have been arranged into five chapters. These are not strictly sequential and actually I encourage you to mix and match the games to suit your own purposes and agenda.

1. 'Jumpstart creative thinking' attempts to illustrate the ideas and principles explained above. The games in this chapter will act as a basis for what follows.
2. 'Jumpstart creative questioning'. Creative questions are those which stimulate an active search for further understanding and/or which encourage reflection upon ideas and meanings. Such questions seek to enrich and inform a child's resource of knowledge.
3. 'Jumpstart creative reasoning'. Some books about thinking skills distinguish between creative and critical kinds of thinking. Creative thinking generates ideas and insights. Critical thinking refines, enriches and sequences information into more logical structures. Practically speaking, creative and critical thinking skills work hand in hand, hence the inclusion of the games in this chapter.
4. 'Jumpstart creative problem solving'. The evolution of human understanding depends as much upon creative insight and intuition as upon logical reasoning. Creative thinking itself is fun and can be undertaken for that purpose alone. But thinking 'outside the box' – going beyond the given – is a powerful complement to solving problems logically.
5. 'Jumpstart creative wordplay'. A huge amount of research indicates that our brains are built to 'do language'. It is an innate ability. The manipulation of symbol and metaphor and the exploration of meaning creatively through language not only helps children to become more effective users of language on a practical day-to-day basis, but aids their understanding of the specialist uses of language across the subject range.

## HOW THE GAMES CAN BE USED

- As starters. Some of the activities can serve to get children 'in the mood' to feel excited about having ideas, asking questions, listening to each other's thoughts, etc. at the start of a lesson, making them ready to engage with the 'meat' of your lesson in the same way.

- Cumulatively. As you explore the book you'll discover that some simpler activities are natural precursors to more complex or sophisticated kinds of thinking. You can link sequences of games together to build up children's creative 'muscles'.
- As bridges between topics and subject areas. Cross-curricular links make knowledge more relevant. Such links are often made at the level of themed content. The theme of *water*, for example, can be explored in Art, Biology, Geography, Music, etc. and this leads to a greater appreciation and understanding on the part of the children. Build on this by taking a creativity game such as 'Question star' (page 52) or 'The 'because' game' (page 73) and applying it in different subjects. This creates a 'thinking link' where diverse content is connected by a common creative strategy.
- As finishers. Sometimes the straightforward transmission of knowledge and ideas forms the core of a lesson. Consolidate children's retention and understanding of lesson content by 'playing with the ideas' using a Jumpstart! game as part of the lesson review or plenary. Playing the same game to open the next lesson helps children to remember what you have told them earlier and to articulate it in their own way, thereby demonstrating their degree of understanding.
- As fillers. I hesitate to suggest that you have any spare time to fill! But if you have, run one of the shorter, simpler creativity games just for the fun of it. Doing this is more valuable than you might at first think – numerous studies have highlighted the connection between humour and fun and the ability to generate creative ideas and insights.

## ADAPTING THE GAMES

The principle of 'going beyond the given' applies here too. Modify and adapt as many of the games in this book as you can to suit your own purposes. In advocating a creative approach I never tell people how to do it but how I do it – in other words, how these activities have worked for me through the years. The games as I've explained them have been effective in many different situations, but you might find that given your circumstances even a slight modification makes all the difference to the productiveness of a technique.

## MATERIALS AND PREPARATION

Most of the activities require minimal preparation and the simplest of materials – pencils, pens and paper (or mini-whiteboards, etc.). Occasionally you will find an activity that asks children to bring in ordinary/household objects. In a few cases an activity requires you and/or the children to prepare sets of cards featuring words and pictures. Some of the games and techniques make use of computers and electronic whiteboards, but you could easily run a paper-based version of these in most cases.

It might be useful to mention here also that while differentiation of materials is sometimes the most effective way of involving all of the children in a mixed-ability class, this is more often not the case in *Jumpstart! Creativity*. Usually a creative thinking activity displays differentiation at the outcome stage: you can launch the same activity with the whole class and each child will perform to his own current level of competence and confidence, as you value that thinking and work to develop those qualities in every child.

Finally, let me emphasise my wish that you'll have as much fun with these games as I think the children will. By doing so you'll be modelling the very attitude – the creative attitude – that you want to instil in them.

# CHAPTER 1

# Jumpstart creative thinking

It is important to realise from the start that creativity is not the gift of the few and it is not the province of the Arts rather than the Sciences. Nor do children need to be academically very able to think creatively in many effective ways. All children are potentially creative: creativity arises from the natural human curiosity that we all possess. It develops from the way that the brain makes basic sense of the world, namely by linking ideas together and by looking at things in many ways. These are the cornerstones of creative thinking.

Creativity is a process. It is a way of actively understanding how the world works. Creativity plays with ideas, generates new ideas and organises and refines them. It uses 'content' – knowledge and facts – as fuel to fire the imagination. Because the world is changing so rapidly in so many ways, it is imperative that we empower our children to inherit the future successfully.

## THE PYRAMID OF CREATIVITY

Several decades of research in the neurosciences and other fields, while not even beginning to solve the 'hard problem' of the nature of consciousness, has given us many valuable insights into how different modes of thinking correlate with activity in the brain. While the technical details of how networks of neurons allow us to express our thoughts are fearsomely complex, the general principles underpinning creative (and critical) thinking are relatively straightforward.

In the 1970s and into the '80s – when I began teaching – creativity was high on the educational agenda. Another and more cynical way of looking at it is that it was fashionable. It was also very unstructured in my experience; loosely defined and lacking the methodologies and rigour (irritating word) that guides the development of thinking skills in children today. In my own field of English, when some free writing was called for, pupils were asked to 'go away and be creative', with the tacit understanding that anything they produced, while being marked for spelling and punctuation etc, would be read with a very lightly critical eye. It was after all, a piece of 'creative' writing and there were no boundaries where that was concerned.

For me this changed when, having instructed a class to write a story, one boy came up to my table after a few minutes and said, 'Sir I don't know what to do,' to which I replied, 'Well just go and think about it.' He considered this briefly and then said, 'But how do I think about it?'

The boy's question changed the direction of my thinking about thinking and has guided the work I've done in developing the hopefully practical ideas and techniques you'll find in this book and others I've written.

We can visualise the principles underlying creative thinking by imagining the 'pyramid of creativity'.

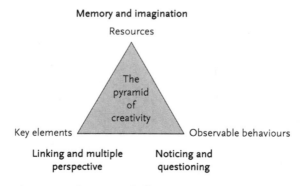

**Figure 1.1:** The pyramid of creativity

First and foremost we have the basic resources of the mind, those of memory and imagination. By memory I do not mean recall, which is our ability to call back into conscious awareness ideas and events that we have experienced in the past. In all of us this is limited to a greater or lesser extent. While creative thinking relies upon recall to some degree, it also taps into the vast amount of subconscious information that all of us possess.

One function of subconscious processing – mental activity that happens outside the realm of our conscious awareness – is to assimilate new 'data' (experiences) into the sense we have up to that point made of the world. This vast network of associations is sometimes called the 'map of reality', though like any map it is not the territory itself but a unique interpretative impression of how we think the world works and how we fit into it.

Much more could be said about this, but suffice to say that the subconscious mind is an incredibly rich and powerful aspect of the thinking we do, one that forms the basis of creativity.

Imagination is the ability we have to draw information from the subconscious, alter it, reconfigure it, evaluate and refine it. In other words we can generate new ideas from information we already possess. Another feature of the imagination is our ability to create mental scenarios that need have nothing to do with our immediate circumstances. We can envision endless possibilities beyond what is happening here and now. This phenomenon expresses itself in what I call 'systematic daydreaming' and reverie. While as educators we appreciate the value of thinking time as a precursor to carrying out all kinds of mental tasks, it is also important to be clear about what kind of thinking we want our pupils to be doing during that time. Deliberate, self-aware daydreaming is one valuable 'tool' we have in our mental toolbox.

Key elements of creative thinking – thinking that generates new associations, ideas and insights – are the facilities we have to link previously disparate thoughts and to look at ideas in different ways (what is often called 'thinking outside the box').

As I've said, the subconscious 'map' is a vast network of associations, continually being enriched by new experiences and knowledge. Many, many techniques exist for facilitating this idea-generating process and, as you will see, many of the activities in this book aim to achieve this.

The points made so far can be summed up in these two principles:

- How many ideas can I have and what use can I make of them?
- To have our best ideas we need lots of ideas.

This first idea makes use of two distinct modes of thinking. To create new ideas and insights we rely on the subconscious mind to 'throw up' material that we had not previously considered. This often takes the form of fresh associations that take us by surprise (which we experience as the well-known 'aha!' moment). It is the basis of the established technique of brainstorming.

This spray of new thoughts forms the raw material that we must then explore and evaluate using different kinds of conscious thinking – speculating, considering different options, refining, reconnecting, judging, coming to conclusions – that we do in order to realise and develop the potential of those ideas.

The second principle highlights the playful and exploratory attitude that nourishes the development of creative thinking skills. When we set children a creative task we encourage them to have ideas in the plural. This not only provides us with more raw material to work on further, but can itself lead to the formation of further linkages between those thoughts.

Creative thinking can and should be enjoyable. Children should feel good when they have new ideas. Thus I emphasise the importance of fostering the attitude of curiosity and playfulness within the creative thinking environment. Children most often display this attitude through the specific behaviours of noticing and questioning. Noticing includes pupils being observant about the world around them and also becoming more aware of their own thinking (known as metacognition). Asking questions feeds the subconscious resource of pre-existing information and sharpens up critical thinking skills as new knowledge is evaluated and incorporated into the sense that children have already made of the world.

In terms of establishing a creative thinking environment, the key concept is –

Flexibility within a structure

In other words, set the children tasks having offered them at least one 'how to' mode of thinking, but without being too prescriptive at this point about outcomes or the quality of the ideas you want them to produce.

Things to do:

Show your class the pyramid of creativity and explain the principles behind creative thinking and what it will 'look like and feel like' when it is happening.

Be explicit about the kinds of thinking the children do. If a pupil, let's say, speculates about what the world might be like in thirty years' time, tell them what they have just done – 'Ah, you're using things you already know to imagine that future world. We can call this speculating or predicting.' If you further ask the pupil why they think the world might be like that, you are asking for them to reason and infer (two important critical thinking skills embedded within a creative thinking context.

And most importantly, model the behaviour. When you set the children a creative thinking task, tackle it yourself and be open about any difficulties you had in completing this. In other words, join in with the fun.

## ALPHA STONES

You will need some small beach pebbles or rounded pieces of polished mineral or glass beads or marbles. The 'alpha' in the title refers to brainwaves produced when we are in a state of 'relaxed alertness'. This is the state of daydream, when the conscious mind is settled so that we can notice ideas and trains of thought coming from 'out of the blue' (actually from the endlessly creative subconscious part of the mind).

Thinking – and noticing what we think – is the precursor to all creative activity. Being able to switch to alpha state at will is a useful mental skill which can be developed through the use of *anchors*. An anchor is a link that is established between a desired behaviour and something over which you have direct conscious control. There are many kinds of anchors; we will explore some of them in this book. An alpha stone is a kinaesthetic (physical/tactile) link that is made between holding the stone and switching to the mental state of relaxed alertness.

Practise with your own alpha stone first. Choose a pebble that looks attractive to you and that sits comfortably in the hand. This will be your stone from now on. If you are right-handed, hold the stone in your left hand. Prepare to feel relaxed and calm – you might have some soothing music playing to help you get into this mood. As you feel yourself settling, put the alpha stone into your right hand. Enjoy the tranquillity. Notice the thoughts streaming effortlessly through your mind. You can guide them gently away from anything to do with worry or the pressures of the day. One good way of doing this is to imagine a pleasant place: whenever negative or unwanted thoughts intrude, deliberately imagine this place – and remember the stone in your hand.

You need spend no more than five minutes a day training yourself to react to the alpha stone. The effects are cumulative – after a few weeks of practice, putting the stone in your hand will immediately create a deep sense of peace and relaxation: your attention will be internalised and you will be able both to notice and to gently guide your trains of thought.

When you have reached this level of skill, introduce alpha stones to your class. Explain their usefulness and emphasise that holding such a stone will help all the children to have lots of good ideas about all sorts of things. You can encourage the children to bring in their own stones, although I always prefer to have a bag of polished pebbles that they can choose from. Once a child has chosen a pebble it will be his particular alpha stone from now on.

Help children to develop the skill of using the stones to anchor the state of relaxed alertness. Practise the technique at different times of the day so that no particular time becomes associated with the desired state. Use the stones in these ways:

- To calm the whole class at the start of the school day/the afternoon session/after a windy breaktime!
- To help individual children settle if they're upset. Take the child aside and have him place the alpha stone in his chosen hand. Encourage him to notice how much better he feels when he does that. *Tip:* The technique is even more effective if you have a calm corner in your room, which acts as a spatial anchor to add to the positive effect of the stone.
- To prepare the children to absorb new information. When in the alpha state we are aware of ideas as they are presented to us and the sense we are making of them. If children don't understand something we've said, they can feel relaxed and self-assured as they express their puzzlement and ask questions. Children's general attitude to knowledge can become one of calm reflectiveness, which is preferable than feeling anxious or nervous over trying to understand and remember.
- To aid memory. When we want children to remember things we've told them, use the alpha stones to establish the state of relaxed alertness as you ask about what they've learned. Because the children are in the same mental state now as when they absorbed the ideas, and can notice their thoughts, they are far more likely to retrieve information than if they were struggling for recall.
- To develop creative thinking. Years ago I started using 'story stones' in my writing workshops. I explained to children that when they held a story stone they could be any character they wanted; they would know everything about that person/ creature and could easily answer any questions asked about him or her (or it). The technique worked brilliantly. I subsequently extended it so that any aspect of a story could be

explored imaginatively. One boy (Y4) decided that he would be a field of wheat. Both his teacher and I wondered what he could possibly say from that point of view . . . But we were soon pleased and astonished when he began talking in the first person about swaying with the wind rather than fighting against it, and how under the sun he grew strong and how under the moon he rested, and how each stalk of wheat allowed the whole field to exist and flourish . . . This was profound and poetical stuff, whether that boy realised it or not!

*Tip*: Children are likely to come to feel that their particular alpha stones are special. If a child loses his stone, make sure you have a larger pebble on your desk. Give the child a new stone and explain that if he touches it to the larger pebble, all the specialness of the old stone will go into the new one. I have found that even many older children will accept this idea.

*Tip*: Find a larger and particularly attractive pebble. Use it as a 'calm stone'. Always keep it in the same place in the classroom. Introduce the idea by saying that whenever you put your hands on the stone you will feel calmness washing through you. Model the technique yourself. Put your hands on the stone and behave as if you are becoming calmer (behaving 'as if' often creates the behaviour in reality). Remember to use the calm stone whenever you feel annoyed or stressed. Tell the children that instead of feeling angry and upset, they can feel much better when they rest their hands on the calm stone. Say too that the more times it's used, the more powerful it becomes and the better it works.

## FOOTPRINTS

This simple activity develops observational skill, deduction, inference and speculation.

- Find pictures of animals' feet and ask children to draw what they think the creatures' footprints would look like. Show video footage of animals walking and running and have the children work out what their tracks would be like.

- Do it the other way round. Show pictures of animal tracks and help children to speculate about what the animals might look like.
- Get the children to draw made-up creatures and monsters. Swap drawings and decide what your creature's footprints would look like.

## CSI – CRIME SCENE INVESTIGATION

This activity extends the skills developed in the 'Footprints' game.

- Develop a scenario with the whole class. For instance:

> The cat burglar finished eating his kebab and rode on his motorbike to the other side of town. Parking the bike on a piece of waste ground, he then walked down the street to the big house on the corner. He waited until the rain shower stopped, then climbed over the mossy old stone wall, walked across the flowerbed and hurried over to the window. The window had a wooden frame. He used a tool [decide what] to lever open the window, damaging the frame in the process. Then he crept into the room and walked across the cream-coloured carpet to the cabinet opposite . . .

- Decide what clues and traces the burglar might leave behind. Have children draw a plan of the garden and room and mark on the evidence. Ask other groups to work out the sequence of events suggested by the evidence.
- Thumbprints. Use an inkpad to collect thumbprints. Give each working group two thumbprints from different people and ask them to notice as many differences as they can.
- Pocket magnifiers. Simple plastic magnifiers are easy and quite cheap to obtain. Have children use them to notice differences between various fibres, seeds and other objects. What differences do children notice between sand grains, salt crystals, sugar crystals?
- Drawing detail. Give the children a leaf of the same sort and ask them to draw it carefully, making sure they include small details that will mark it out from every other leaf in the class.

## THE DETECTIVE GAME

Asking children to sift through clues to answer a question or solve a puzzle allows them to practise a number of both creative and critical thinking skills. You can start with a short list of clues and simply ask, 'What do you think could have happened?'

For example:

1. Kevin Gentry has had a valuable pendant stolen from his home.
2. The pendant was kept in the top drawer of a Welsh dresser in Kevin Gentry's front room.
3. There are muddy shoe prints in the hallway.
4. It has been raining since early morning.
5. A number of final demands for unpaid bills are lying on the hallway table.
6. John Toff, Kevin Gentry's nephew, is spending a week at the house.
7. The glass of one of the window panels in the front room is smashed.
8. The drawers of the Welsh dresser have been wrenched out and their contents thrown on the floor.
9. Fragments of glass are scattered on the carpet in the front room.
10. An ornament cabinet in the front room is undisturbed.
11. There are shoe prints in the flower border.
12. The front room window is made up of eight small panels.
13. Kevin Gentry said he saw someone in a hoodie running away from the house.

There are a few possible solutions to this mystery:

- Kevin Gentry might have staged the robbery to claim on the insurance.
- John Toff might have stolen the pendant from his uncle, for reasons unknown.
- A thief might have broken in and stolen the pendant.

If children come up with one of these scenarios, or some of their own, ask them to examine the clues again carefully to check for contradictions or anomalies. For instance:

The front room window is made of eight small panels, yet only one is smashed. How could a thief have climbed through such a small opening?

(Astute children might ask *which* panel is smashed. Is it one that would allow a thief to put his or her hand through to unlatch or unlock the window?)

The fact that the pendant was hidden in the top drawer of the Welsh dresser, and that only the dresser was disturbed, suggests that the thief knew of the pendant's hiding place.

It has been raining since early morning and there are muddy footprints in the hallway. This suggests that the person who left footprints in the flower border could be the person who left the muddy prints in the hallway, pointing the finger of guilt at Kevin Gentry or his nephew.

(Again, a perceptive child might suggest checking the shoe sizes and sole patterns of the suspects with the prints left in the flowerbed.)

Kevin Gentry's claim that he saw a hooded figure running away is not backed up by any proof.

The fact that there are a number of final demands for unpaid bills on the hallway table suggests that Kevin Gentry is short of money. Perhaps he, maybe in collusion with his nephew, staged the theft to claim on the insurance.

This is a very simple mystery and the finger of guilt points towards Kevin Gentry, perhaps aided by his nephew.

Take it further:

If the children could interview the suspects, what questions would they ask (bearing in mind that Gentry and Toff could lie)?

Ask groups to invent further clues to implicate a new character in the theft.

Ask groups to invent further scenarios:

Write a single-sentence overview of what has happened.

Invent a few suspects.

Discuss and visualise the scene in more detail.

Create some clues that implicate one or more of the characters.

Even in this simple version of the detective game children are making creative links between pieces of information, speculating, inferring and reasoning, and noticing possible contradictions.

You can increase the difficulty of the task by increasing the number of clues, together with their attendant anomalies and contradictions. Table 1.1 shows a more complex and ambiguous scenario.

Again, what could have happened? Various stories are suggested by the clues. Maybe Steven Phillips killed Ben Leech and hid his body (burying it using the spade?) – perhaps out of sheer dislike of the man, or maybe because Phillips owed Leech money (though this is speculation, with no supporting evidence). Another possibility is that Steven Phillips took his family to New Zealand without telling anyone, to escape his presumed debts. Maybe Leech lent or gave him money to accomplish this.

Ask children to find clues that support these scenarios, plus any others they invent for themselves.

Ask groups to pick one scenario and then create further clues to support it *but not definitively prove it*.

Note that this is an opportunity to explain ideas like the 'red herring' in murder mystery stories, fragments of information that have no bearing on the actual crime, or that lead detectives along a mistaken route.

**Table 1.1:** Detective game grid

| | | | | | |
|---|---|---|---|---|---|
| A cold cup of tea is on the side table in the lounge. | Ten years ago the garden shed burned down. | The number of the house is 42. | An empty milk bottle stands on the kitchen worktop. | There is a week's worth of mail on the hallway floor. | The TV is on standby. |
| The DVD machine records the same programme each week. | Ben Leech won the lottery two years ago. | There is an oil stain on the drive. | The boxroom upstairs is always kept locked. | The children's school is two miles away. | The Phillips family lives here. |
| Flowers in the front room have died. | A telephone number has been scrawled on the wall by the phone. | Steven Phillips had a plumbing business that went bankrupt. | Ben Leech is a bachelor and a recluse. | Mrs. Phillips collects stamps and old books. | The son is 12 years old. |
| The spare house key is missing from the hook in the hallway. | There is a week's worth of newspapers by the bed. | The bed in the main bedroom is unmade. | There are five messages on the telephone answering machine. | A bottle of milk in the kitchen has gone sour. | The lock on the garden shed has been forced. |
| A guidebook to New Zealand lies on the coffee table in the front room. | Neighbours say the family keeps itself to itself. | The family owns a very valuable pedigree cat. | There is no money in a tin on the mantelpiece in the lounge. | Ben Leech, whom Steven Phillips knew at school, called round three weeks ago. | A faded red stain can be seen on the stair carpet. |
| Ben Leech's car has been in a long-stay car park for almost three weeks. | Three pink rose bushes and a red one grow in the back garden. | Steven Phillips and Ben Leech were enemies at school. | There are fresh footprints in the flower border. | Neighbours have not seen the Phillips' cat for nearly three weeks. | Recently Steven Phillips bought a spade from the local ironmonger. |

These activities ask children to speculate. Point out that this is not the same as jumping to conclusions. Speculations are possible scenarios based on no or little evidence – another name for speculating is 'maybe-thinking'. Incidentally, the word derives from Latin meaning 'to look from a vantage point', which in turn comes from *specula*, meaning 'watchtower'. Jumping to a conclusion means making a judgement or making a decision in the absence of any or many facts.

For example, ask children to decide what's happening here:

Children who simply say 'One person is pushing another' are simply observing what they see. Those who engage in maybe-thinking, saying 'Maybe the person on the left is being bullied' are speculating. Any child who says definitely what's going on – 'The one on the left is being bullied' – has jumped to a conclusion.

Highlight the difference by asking for a range of possibilities. 'OK, so maybe one person is bullying the other, or . . .?' Challenge the class to come up with at least five ideas.

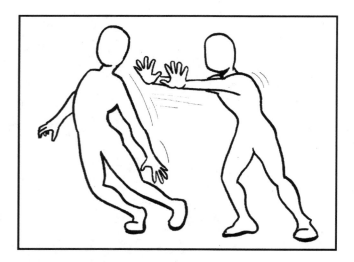

**Figure 1.2:** Jumping to conclusions

*Tip*: Since in these activities groups of children or the whole class are asked to discuss clues and scenarios, you can take the opportunity to do a discussion analysis.

> How was the group organised? Did one person take charge?

> Did anyone dominate the group, or did you all have an equal say?

> Who gave reasons for their theories or conclusions? (i.e. used 'because'.)

> Did anyone want to say something but decided not to? If so, why? (Individuals might want to ponder this privately.)

> Have you learned anything that would make you better detectives next time?

For more activities in the style of 'The detective game' see 'CSI – Crime Scene Investigation' on page 9 and 'How Relevant' in my *Jumpstart! Thinking Skills and Problem Solving*.


## THEME COLLAGE

The aim is to produce a multisensory collage on a theme. General abstract themes work best if philosophical discussion is to be one of the outcomes. So if you choose the theme of 'time', for example, help children to explore the following:

- What things do we normally associate with time? (clocks, time-tables, age, the rush hour, change, time-lapse pictures, special times like anniversaries).
- What phrases and sayings come to mind when we think of time? (time and tide wait for no man/a stitch in time saves nine/the Seven Ages of Man/the moving finger writes and having writ moves on/I'm late, I'm late for a very important date . . . ).
- What stories, pieces of art, etc. explore the notion of time? (*Dr Who*, *The Picture of Dorian Gray* [Oscar Wilde], *The Time Machine* [H.G. Wells], Salvador Dali's melting clocks, etc.).

- What comes to mind when we think of time in relation to subjects taught at school? (the seasons, history and timelines, cooking times for food, geological ages, time and space, Albert Einstein – light years, double time in music, keeping time in dance).

*Tip*: This is a good opportunity to practise mind-mapping skills with the children.

Now discuss with the class what specific pictures, objects, words might be used to create the collage. Once it has been made, use it as a springboard for exploring further ideas:

- How could we explain the notion of time to someone who knew nothing about it, without referring to clocks and timetables and the things we usually associate with time?
- What if you could freeze time and do all you wanted to do in the space of a second?
- What if you had a time machine like the traveller in H.G. Wells's famous story and could go to one time in the past and one time in the future?
- What if there was a world where, when people were born, they were given a 'bag of time' to spend or share or squander as they pleased?

*Note*: If you want to learn more about exploring concepts philo-sophically with your class, you could start with the following books:

Stanley, S. and Bowkett, S. *But Why?: Developing Philosophical Thinking in the Classroom*, London: Network Educational Press, 2004.
Law, S. *The Philosophy Files*, London: Orion, 2002.
Law, S. *The Philosophy Files 2*, London: Orion, 2006.

## THE INKBLOT GAME

You will need watercolour paints or coloured inks and sheets of paper.

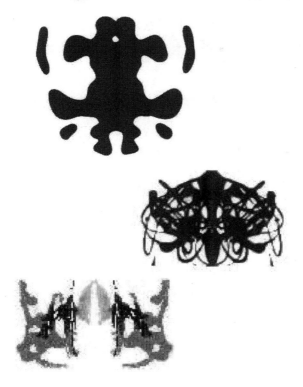

**Figure 1.3:** The inkblot game

Many people know about the famous Rorschach or 'inkblot' test where shapes, patterns and objects can be discerned in splodges of ink or paint as in Figure 1.3. We can use the technique to help develop children's creativity.

To make an inkblot take a sheet of paper and fold it in half, then open it out and cover one half with a protective second sheet. Use inks or paints to make random patterns on the exposed half of the sheet. Remove the protective sheet and fold the original, so reproducing the pattern.

- Have children pass the inkblot sheets round. List the shapes that different children discern. Later, show the inkblots to the whole class and point out the great variety of shapes hidden in them. This gives every child the experience of looking at the inkblots in many ways. Being able to take different viewpoints is a powerful aspect of creative thinking. More implicitly the children will come to understand that everything has potential, that many ideas can be contained within a simple resource and that not all of them are visible at the start.

- I've visited schools where coloured inkblot sheets were made into paper butterfly mobiles and kites.
- Use a number of inkblot sheets to help children make up stories. List the objects and animals seen in the inkblots and use them as characters, settings and events in a narrative.
- Use the inkblots synaesthetically. See 'What colour is this music?' on page 40.

## WHAT COULD IT BE?

This is an interpretation game. Find pictures of ambiguous designs, of antique implements, medical instruments, scientific apparatus, etc. and ask children to discuss what these things might be used for. Guide the group as necessary by focussing their attention on particular parts of the chosen objects.

An internet search usually brings up plenty of images that you can use. Another good source is *The Ultimate Visual Dictionary*, reissued regularly by Dorling Kindersley.

A variation of this game is to look at simple everyday implements and gadgets and to work out and discuss why they are so designed. These insights might be obvious to us as adults, but children need to be given some opportunity to make such discoveries for themselves to develop their creativity.

## HEATH ROBINSON MACHINES

William Heath Robinson (1872–1944) was an English cartoonist and illustrator often remembered for his drawings of highly complicated gadgets and machines that were used for the simplest and most ridiculous purposes, such as automatically cooking and serving a fried breakfast or putting up wallpaper. So-called Heath Robinson contraptions were intentionally ironic and funny, although the logic behind them was usually sound and one could easily imagine such contraptions actually working – if anyone could be bothered to build them!

- Find a selection of Heath Robinson contraptions in books or from the internet. Use them to help children understand the function of cogs, pulleys, drive belts and other component parts.
- Brainstorm a list of ordinary everyday tasks such as putting the cat out at night, polishing shoes, cleaning teeth, showering, combing hair, etc. Use Heath Robinson's principle of making contraptions as complicated as possible for designing machines to carry out these functions. Challenge children to explain why their designs would actually work.
- Contrast this by looking at the design of actual gadgets and implements. Help children to appreciate the principle of simplicity and the power behind economy of design.

## CONCEPT FLAGS

When children appreciate symbolism they have taken an important step forward in their understanding of the world. A symbol is a representation, usually visual, of a complex weave of ideas whose power and significance often grow over time. A symbol can be taken as a kind of shorthand for concepts that reach beyond the symbol itself. A sign, on the other hand, is a simplification of one or more ideas (we speak of traffic signs, for instance, and not traffic symbols).

- Begin to develop children's understanding of symbols by looking first at signs. Traffic signs, company logos, product logos, safety signs and team logos are easily accessible and provide a useful area of discussion around the notion of representation.
- Explore how certain animals have come to represent abstract qualities. Look at familiar similes as a way of introducing this. Most children will have heard 'as sly as a fox', 'as playful as a kitten' and 'as brave as a lion'. Look then at how certain animals

have come to represent something more. What, for instance, could Aslan the lion represent in C.S. Lewis's famous *Chronicles of Narnia*? Look at the way animals are portrayed in heraldry, where their particular positioning is an important feature of their overall significance.

- Look at animals in mythology and the way in which some animals have come to represent different things in different cultures. The dragon is a clear example of this. Discuss the Christian story of St George and the Dragon with the children. On one level it is an exciting adventure tale, but looked at symbolically it takes on a new and more powerful dimension. Find other myths that have left traces of themselves in our everyday lives. What does a heart with an arrow through it mean, for example?

- Consider engaging boys' interest more by looking at famous monsters in literature. Most, if not all boys will be familiar with vampires. The symbology of this image has changed greatly over the past hundred years or so and, partly thanks to Bram Stoker's influential novel *Dracula* and the many related films that have followed, the vampire has now come to represent parasitism, bloodlust and a longing for normal existence. Mary Shelley's *Frankenstein* monster symbolises mankind's crude tampering with the basic forces of life (the 'spark' of life, as we say), and also the way in which what is different is feared and shunned. The monster itself represents a vain and pitiful search for identity and comes to symbolise the outsider who is never accepted. In philosophy a zombie is a creature that is indistinguishable from a human being except that it has no mind or sense of self-awareness. Thinking of zombies in this way helps philosophers to discuss concepts such as identity and consciousness (see, for instance, Law, S. *The Philosophy Gym*, London: Headline Books, 2003).

- Use any or all of the above as preparation for making 'concept flags'. Choose a theme such as bravery, honour, ambition and help the children to decide what could represent these ideas, and why. Images can be drawn or items of clip art may be printed. Add a more kinaesthetic element by using physical objects such as leaves, coloured threads and strings, pieces of material, feathers, etc. Explore with the children why the colours, relative sizes and positioning of these images on the flag will be significant. There are many variations of this basic activity:

- Design a new school logo. If your school already has a badge, what do its elements represent? What other images could symbolise the qualities and aspirations of the school?
- Create a new shield or logo for a favourite sports team.
- Design a personal flag that sums up one's qualities and ideals.
- Create a family flag that says something about the family's history.
- Design a flag to symbolise the current year or decade.

## THE CRISS-CROSS GAME

This game gives children practice in the creative thinking activity of brainstorming and helps them to realise that all of their ideas are valued. Brainstorming is sometimes called 'ideas cascade'. Once the game starts, every idea and suggestion should be recorded without being analysed or judged, written briefly on the board or a flip chart by one or more scribes or video- or audio-taped for later discussion and analysis.

Criss-cross is a particular version of the basic brainstorming activity. It is very focussed insofar as the two objects used can be subject-specific or relevant to a particular topic you are working on.

- Choose two items to begin with. You can simply name these, or you might want to have visuals for the children to look at. We'll use a TV and a pen as an example.
- Begin by saying 'What do you get [or 'What might happen'] if you cross a TV set with a pen?' There will probably be a great rush of suggestions to begin with and then they will tail off. Don't worry if there are silences between suggestions: let the game run its course, but if you see children struggling to force ideas, you can end the activity, prompt the children in some way or introduce a third object.

Here are some of the suggestions made by a Y5 group I worked with:

- A pen with a tiny built-in TV set. You can watch cartoons while you're pretending to do your homework.

- A TV with an interactive screen that you can write on.
- A TV programme that teaches you how to spell. It's connected to the pen and actually guides your hand over the paper (or interactive paper).
- A pen that's also a computer. If you make a spelling mistake, it will tell you so, politely of course.
- A pen linked to a computer database and a TV. When you write a story a signal goes to the database and the computer creates a cartoon or CGI (computer-generated imagery) version of your story.
- Or, using the same idea, if you drew a machine, the computer would show you a moving version of your machine on the TV.
- Instead of a pen, how about surgical instruments? The TV-computer would help you to operate and guide your hand.

These were some of the more intriguing of a large crop of ideas generated by the class over the course of ten minutes. The only prompting the children needed was my suggestion that 'TV' could also be a computer monitor/electronic whiteboard. I then introduced a third object, a clock, and these were some of the children's suggestions:

- A pen with a little screen that tells you the time anywhere in the world.
- A pen connected to the internet. Once you've written a letter, the pen remembers it and emails it to anyone you like.
- You could be 'instant penpals' with people anywhere in the world. (One child then suggested that countries that wanted to keep their citizens in the dark about what was going on elsewhere wouldn't be able to do so now. That started a discussion about how to smuggle such pens into these countries, but I said we'd leave that for another time.)
- A computer-pen that could do a version of 'predictive texting'. It would guess what you wanted to write and (a) guide your hand over the paper, (b) make the words appear ahead of itself on interactive paper, or (c) make suggestions for phrasing things in a better way.

What astonishes me time and time again when I play this game is the quality of the ideas that many children produce. In a world that is changing so quickly on so many fronts, it is vital that children should not only be unafraid of ideas and the pace of change, but have the ability to make a useful contribution themselves to that change.

*Extension*: Once you have a stock of suggestions, you can discuss with your group how they can be made to work (the suggestions, not the children). How would a pen that offered you suggestions for spelling, punctuation, grammar, etc. actually work? There are good opportunities here to introduce science, technology and design into the game.

## PROBLEM SOLVER GRID

The principle of 'How many ideas can I have and what use can I make of them?' (page 4) is exemplified in the grid on page 24. Using a 6x6 grid allows for the use of dice rolls to select items randomly, and it is well known in the field of thinking skills that the inclusion of randomness and chance enriches the creative process in the generation of fresh ideas and connections. (I believe it was the writer/ inventor Edward de Bono who highlighted this notion. He also said that creativity involved breaking out of established patterns so that you could look at things in new ways.)

The 'inventions grid' occurred to me when a teacher friend came to me with a problem. He had set his Y9 design class the task of designing a handy new household gadget. The problem was that most of the students were having trouble thinking of a new idea for a gadget that they could then draw and label. I had used 6×6 grids before in the context of creative writing[1], so the inventions grid was just an extension of that technique.

The household objects in the grid shown in Figure 1.4 give focus to the task, while the more ambiguous images allow for the 'creative space' necessary to think in terms of ideas, plural, rather than one idea as an outcome. Note also that the grid is true to the principle of 'flexibility within a structure', which prevents the creative process

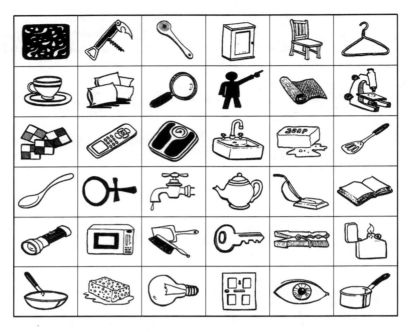

**Figure 1.4:** Inventions grid

being too open and woolly; if it was, children might flounder in the absence of a definite procedure supporting their thinking.

You might need to remind children of the process of going 'along the corridor and up the stairs' during their dice rolls – though using this or another 6x6 grid is an ideal opportunity to introduce the concept of co-ordinates.

The activity can be run with the whole class, with children in groups or pairs, or working alone. Two items need to be selected from the grid by rolling the die. Explain to the class that they are not to *try* to think of an idea, but simply to notice what pops into mind, given the intention to have an idea for a new household gadget or device. In other words, the 'see it and say it' technique of brainstorming. Also explain that if an idea doesn't come to mind, rather than struggle to think of something, children should roll the die again to select two new items. As with many activities and techniques used to develop creativity, most children will find that this becomes easier and more effective with practice. In many people 'routine thinking' or thinking inside the box limits creativity but, given time, the creative flow of ideas can be turned on at will.

Here are a few examples of new gadgets, or variations on ones already existing, using the grid shown in Figure 1.4. I recommend trying out the technique yourself before launching it in the classroom.

> 5/3 vacuum cleaner – 3/3 tap. First thoughts – separate chambers in the bag to suck up liquid spills and dry fluff, dust etc. Maybe a flexible hose attachment for the liquids. A vacuum pump that sucks rainwater into a vessel (from gutters and water butts) that cleans and filters it for washing and, if technically possible, drinking. A vacuum arrangement linked to a face mask to filter out smog and other particulates in the air.

> 6/4 spatula – 2/3 ambiguous object (reminds me of the Egyptian symbol of life, the Ankh). First thoughts – the Ankh image also reminds me of some kind of multi purpose tool or a universal key. A kitchen implement with several functions . . . (Ideas dry up at this point, so I move on.)

> 3/2 dustpan and brush – 3/4 weighing scales. First thoughts – dustpan and brush as an example of something that collects, gathers. The scales measure. How about a device that measures pollutants in the air, including things that can trigger allergic reactions so that people with sensitivities and intolerances to things like animal hair and pollen can be forewarned. Further, a measuring device like a food probe that can detect possible allergens in food, say when you're eating out.

The inventions grid also emphasises the principle that 'To have my best ideas I need to have lots of ideas.' When I use the grid in thinking workshops, out of all of the ideas thrown up during the course of the activity there are usually a few that are quite novel and, occasionally, one that seems truly original.

(As a side issue, while originality is often the desired outcome of creative thinking, bear in mind that, as children learn, they may come up with an idea that they have thought of for the first time – i.e. they have made a fresh connection in their imagination – but in the wider world the idea may be quite commonplace. Indeed, the 'gadgets' I thought of above may already exist.)

A more sophisticated use of the grid is as a problem solver in a more general sense, by thinking of the images metaphorically as well as literally. So for instance, rolling 3/3 we again get a tap. Thinking more broadly we can say that it is an example of a device that 'delivers on demand'. That same definition would fit the internet, which delivers information at our fingertips. Another common feature of the internet is that, over time, often-visited websites (I'm thinking particularly of online retailers) 'learn' our preferences in music, films, books etc. and so guide and advise us as to what else is out there that might be of interest. So here we have information delivered on demand that becomes increasingly refined according to our preferences. We might say that in using the internet we tap into a reservoir, or more accurately an ocean, of information just about whenever we want it. (Ripple, splash, drip feed, depths, currents etc.) Future refinements of the technology might see each of us going through life with a device that comes to 'know' what we want to learn, what our aspirations are, what our fears or anxieties might be: a device that responds to our voices, body language, other more subtle physiological signals and, perhaps, ultimately, our very thoughts. A kind of AI personal mentor . . .

Note that the above amounts to the ponderings that were triggered by my thinking more generally and metaphorically about tap – tapping into – reservoir – flow. (As we grow sensitive to the metaphors that weave themselves through our language, we cannot help but become more keenly aware of how they are often used in rhetorical and emotive ways to try and persuade us towards a certain point of view. At the time of writing, the media are awash with tap-related metaphors about Britain leaving the EU. So in the context of immigration we read of floods of incomers, stemming the tide, reducing the drain on our resources, a deluge of rules and regulations, ripples of alarm on the stock market, drawing lines in the sand etc.)

Using the grid as a problem-solving tool goes like this:

> First clearly define the problem that you wish to resolve. This might be a personal issue, one related to your classroom, the whole school, the country or the world. When using the technique with children, it's wise to choose wider issues that won't have too much of a personal emotional component.
>
> Maintain a clear expectation that your creativity will generate ideas.
>
> Roll the die twice to select an image from the grid, with the intention that this will give you further insights into the nature of the issue and/or a partial or complete strategy for solving the problem.
>
> Be prepared to engage in what's often called stream-of-consciousness thinking (another water metaphor!).
>
> If the image selected doesn't begin to generate ideas for you within a few seconds, select a second image and brainstorm connections between them, with the expectation that this richer source of information will further aid the creative process. *Do not* keep on rolling the die to select further images, as this will swamp you and muddy the waters of your thinking.
>
> Write your thoughts down.

*Tip*: Even if the flow of ideas dwindles to a trickle and then dries up, come back to your notes later. In the meantime you will be subconsciously assimilating information and focussing on the problem at hand. You might well find that further insights bubble up out of the blue that could take you another step forward in finding a solution to the issue.

As an example:

I want some ideas about improving my time management. I have lots of jobs to do and I'm not sure how to prioritise them . . .

> 6/5 microscope. First thoughts – Maybe I'm trying to tackle some of the work in too much detail. I could save time by leaving out some of the less relevant aspects. Perhaps I'm

focussing in on smaller tasks at the expense of larger ones. In other words, my field of view is too narrow. If I pulled back to get an overview of what needs to be done I might get a clearer idea of the order in which things need to be done. Also, bearing in mind that when I look through a microscope my attention is focussed entirely on what I see through the lens, I could take a look at the 'wider world' to realise that this work is just one part of my life.

I had an argument with a friend and want to know the best way of rebuilding bridges . . .

3/1 light bulb. First thoughts – Friendships, like light bulbs, can be fragile. I recognise that I was being too heavy-handed in discussing some topics on which we disagree. In mending things with my friend I need to handle the matter carefully, and I must certainly not make light of it! I also see more clearly that my friend's reaction could be because of a self-esteem issue – maybe this is the central element of the problem.

But how best to make up?

4/3 teapot. First thoughts – Invite him round for tea? Meet on neutral ground such as at a coffee shop? Tea is an ordinary everyday thing, so when we meet I'll keep the conversation focussed on everyday topics. Some people put the milk in the cup first so that the hot tea doesn't crack the glaze. I'll moderate my views on some topics I get heated about.

I'm reminded of an old story of the emperor who wanted the advice of a much-esteemed wise man. Out of deference, the emperor agreed to meet in the wise man's favourite tea shop. 'So how can I help you sir?' the wise man said, whereupon the emperor began to prattle on about how *he* thought various important matters of state should be tackled. Nodding politely, the wise man poured tea for the emperor, and kept pouring so that the liquid spilled over into the saucer. When the emperor complained about this the wise man said, 'Lord, like this cup, you are too full of your own opinions. Empty your mind of them and then I will advise you.'

Strategy – Keep my opinions to myself!

# BIG IT UP, SHRINK IT DOWN

This is a thinking game that can be used with many of the other activities in this book. The idea is to take a concept, an object, a situation, etc. and enlarge as many aspects of it as you can think of. Then, as the flow of ideas begins to slow down, look at it in a different way and shrink or reduce those aspects. So, for example:

### The story of Cinderella

Big it up!

- The many adventures of Cinderella.
- Cinderella's nasty stepmother gives her a much bigger list of chores than usual.
- Cinderella has four cruel stepsisters.
- After dancing at the ball Cinders' feet swell up so the glass slipper won't fit!
- The Prince is mega rich and owns palaces in every city in the land.
- Cinderella is actually already rich and is pretending to be a downtrodden drudge just to see what some of her subjects have to go through.

Shrink it down!

- The prince is a fraudster and is actually just an ordinary boy from down the street.
- The sisters' evil fairy godmother puts a spell on the slipper so it starts to get smaller.
- Write the story of Cinderella as a 'mini adventure' of no more than 100 words.
- Cinders' fairy godmother has inflated her magical powers. In fact she can only grant one tiny wish per month.
- The fairy godmother only has 'shrinking magic' that makes things smaller or less powerful.
- Create a 30-second advert for selling glass slippers.

### An ice-cream van

Big it up!

- An ice-cream van that always offers lots of flavours.
- A mobile grocery van that sells hundreds of different things.
- An automatic ice-cream delivery service that runs on narrow gauge rails connecting every town and village.
- Ice-cream made with many more and different ingredients so kids would enjoy getting a balanced diet.
- Ice-cream vans that also delivered the mail.
- Ice-cream vans that carried passengers too, so people who had no cars could still get around. (Ice-cream buses! So how about coffee-morning buses where people could meet for a chat? Or a school-in-a-van that delivered lessons to children who were at home ill or injured?)

Shrink it down!

- An ice-cream pill to which you just add milk to make instant ice-cream.
- Ice-cream sweets that you buy in sealed cold-bags.
- Ice-cream peddlers who carry their wares in backpack-coolers.

'Big it up, shrink it down' is a thinking tool for generating ideas rather than evaluating them for practicality. It exploits the creative principle that to have our best ideas, we need to have lots of ideas.

## ODD-ONE-OUT-AND-IN

Traditionally 'Odd-one-out' is an exercise that highlights classification and reasoning. Used conventionally the activity relies upon children's general knowledge and, at worst, can simply descend into a 'guess the right answer' kind of experience, which may well induce anxiety.

Pick the odd-one-out in the following list and give a reason for your choice:

- rose, daffodil, tulip, cauliflower, crocus, Altona.

Perhaps you chose cauliflower because it is a vegetable, maybe guessing that Altona is a flower because so are rose, daffodil and tulip. Good answer, with a strong reason attached to it. But it is not the only answer. Take a more creative approach: can you now think of any other reasons for choosing cauliflower as the odd-one-out?

- Cauliflower is the only edible item on the list (as far as I know!).
- Cauliflower is not usually grown for its appearance, although sometimes you see very attractive ornamental cauliflowers.
- You do not find cauliflowers in a florist's.
- The word cauliflower is more of a description than the other items. The roots of the word (pardon the pun) mean 'cabbage-flower', but there is also an etymological thread to 'stem' (Latin: *caulis*, stem, cabbage).
- Cauliflower is the only item on the list with all of the vowels in its name.

Extend the activity by deliberately thinking about why each of the other items could reasonably be the odd-one-out.

- Rose, because it's also a past tense verb.
- Rose, because it's also used as a girl's name (although maybe Altona is, too – though I hope not cauliflower!).
- Rose, because it's the only one-syllable word in the list.
- Rose, because it's also the name of a colour.
- Daffodil, because it's the only word with the same letter appearing twice in a row.
- Tulip, because it's almost a homophone of 'two lips'. (A homophone is a word that is pronounced the same as another but has a different meaning.)
- Crocus, because the first syllable is also the shortened name of a dangerous reptile.
- Altona, because it's the only example with a capitalised first letter.

- Altona, because it's the only item in the list I'd never heard of previously.
- Altona, because it has the same letter at the start and the end.
- Altona, because it's a sub-category and not a general term (it's a variety of hydrangea – I had to look that up!).

Already we can see that the activity is now far richer in ideas and uses a greater diversity of thinking skills. It's also more fun and helps to take away the fear of the wrong answer. Notice how the use of levity helps to set the emotional tone of the game. It's about playing with ideas and establishing fertile soil for developing creative thinkers (if not for growing cauliflowers).

- Extend the game further by adding other lists:

  1. rose, daffodil, tulip, cauliflower, crocus, Altona.
  2. town, city, village, Utopia, park, suburb.
  3. tea, coke, juice, beer, water, coffee.
  4. carpenter, miner, teacher, electrician, baker, barber.
  5. ant, bear, cat, deer, eel, fox.
  6. France, Germany, London, Italy, Sweden, Spain.

- Pick a list and sequence the items in various ways:

  o By size, smallest to largest, or largest to smallest.
  o In alphabetical order.
  o By number of syllables.
  o By cost, rarity, popularity.

- Prioritise in terms of usefulness to people.
- Prioritise, adding personal opinion. Rank the occupations in list 4 in order of how important you think they are to society. Put the items in list 1 in the order in which you'd like to see them growing in your garden.
- Play 'odd-one-in'. List the characteristics that all the items in a list have in common, then add further examples with:

  o All of those characteristics.
  o Some of those characteristics.
  o One shared characteristic.

This is a good opportunity to introduce or revisit Venn diagrams, mind mapping and other visual organisers of information.

- Pick two items from any two lists and put them together in a sentence: 'My teacher has a vase of daffodils on her desk.' Increase the challenge by choosing three items to use in a sentence, then four items . . .

**Table 1.2:** Odd-one-out-and-in

| rose | daffodil | tulip | cauliflower | crocus | Altona |
|------|----------|-------|-------------|--------|--------|
| town | city | village | Utopia | park | suburb |
| tea | coke | juice | beer | water | coffee |
| carpenter | miner | teacher | electrician | baker | barber |
| ant | bear | cat | deer | eel | fox |
| France | Germany | London | Italy | Sweden | Spain |

- Randomise the game. Dropping the items in a 6×6 grid as in Table 1.2 (remembering the rule for co-ordinates – along the corridor and up the stairs), 'juice' is three along and four up, 'suburb' is 6/5, 'miner' is 2/3. Now roll dice to choose two items and put them in a sentence – 5/5 'park' and 2/5 'city'. That's easy – 'In the middle of the city there is a beautiful park'. Now roll the dice once more – three. Can you think of three other sentences using 'city' and 'park'?

  o It's hard to park in the city.
  o 'CityParks' is a new leisure venture where green play and rest areas are created on the flat roofs of office blocks.
  o 'New Parks' is a southern suburb of the city. Notice that in this last example I used a third item from my grid (suburb). Increase the challenge of the game further by using more than two randomly chosen items in a sentence.

*Tip*: Add a kinaesthetic element to the game by asking the children to draw pictures of the featured items, or use clip art and either print and paste onto a paper grid, or practise computer skills by creating grids electronically.

### Odd-one-out snap

Make a set of cards using items similar to the examples we've already explored. Children work in pairs or groups of two or three. Each child is dealt a similar number of cards. The first child puts down a card. The second child adds a card. Whichever child in the group makes a reasonable link between them wins both cards and puts them aside in a treasure trove. So:

> Child 1 puts down 'baker'.
>
> Child 2 puts down 'deer'.
>
> One of the children says 'Both words end in "er" ', and so wins both cards.

Note that the game encourages more than putting both words into a sentence. The game can be made more challenging if the children resist making a link that's been noticed between two cards and wait until a third or even a fourth card is put down. Making links becomes more difficult as the number of cards increases, but of course the reward is greater.

## SENSORY JOURNEY

Metacognition is the mental skill of noticing one's own thoughts and being able to modify those thoughts on reflection. Developing metacognitive skill is vital in helping children to become more creative and more effective thinkers.

One quick and simple way of achieving this is to take children on a *sensory journey*. This is a visualisation that you can either script in advance in greater or lesser detail, or improvise as you go along. Sensory journeys can be run as a whole-group activity, or you can work more intensively on a one-to-one basis. When children have some experience of such visualisations they can usually create more for themselves quite easily. Here are a few ideas to try:

### A trip around the school

Ask the children to close their eyes or stare at a blank space on the wall, or down at the tabletop. Have the children imagine that they are going to stand up and walk out of the classroom. Tell them to turn left in their minds (or right, depending on the layout of the school!). Say:

> Now keep walking until you come to the hall. Another class is having a PE lesson. Notice the sounds they make. Notice how the sounds echo around the hall. There is a blue sponge ball, about the size of a tennis ball, lying at your feet. Pick up the ball and squeeze it. Feel the sponginess of the ball. Open up your hand and notice how the sponge ball returns to its original shape. Bring the ball up to your nose and smell the spongy rubbery smell . . . Now do a bit of magic and pretend the ball turns into an apple. Notice how the smell changes. Notice how the weight changes – it's heavier now and it feels different too. You can either keep the fruit to eat later or turn it back into a sponge ball and bounce it hard on the floor. Count how many times it bounces before it comes to a stop . . .

Running a visualisation of this kind will also develop many children's concentration span as they continue to explore their own thoughts. The trick is to vary what you ask the children to notice. Make sure that you engage all of the senses in the visualisation, and keep it interesting and good fun by introducing 'bits of magic' like turning the ball into fruit.

*Tip*: Make it clear to the group that if any of them feel uncomfortable during the activity, they can open their eyes at any time. If they do this, encourage them to read a book. This will take their mind off whatever it was that bothered them, but means that the child is sitting quietly while the rest of the group continues with the visualisation.

In the version of the activity above, the children remain silent while you guide the visualisation. You can of course ask for feedback from individuals as the visualisation continues. So as the group all notice the blue sponge ball you can say 'Now do a bit of magic and pretend the ball turns into a piece of fruit. Emily, you choose the fruit we will imagine . . .'

The value of this variation is that *you* don't have to have all the ideas. You will also benefit metacognitively yourself, because as you guide the children you will be having the visualisation too. Emily's sudden announcement of 'a giant blackberry' adds variety and delightful surprise to your own sensory journey.

A more subtle benefit is that when Emily momentarily breaks her state of concentration to speak, as she returns to her world of imagination she will likely be more focussed on her thoughts. These may also be more vivid to her now. It's a bit like interrupting yourself in silent reading: taking your eyes away from the page for a few seconds allows you to return refreshed and with renewed concentration.

**Pair work**

**Figure 1.5:** Sensory journey map

Children can work in twos on sensory journeys. One child might guide the visualisation while the other experiences it, or the children can talk it through together. A simple map helps them to organise their thoughts and keep track of their journey. Look at Figure 1.5 opposite, an imaginary town. Encourage the children to pick a place to start – let's say they choose the spot at the edge of the park at the northern end of Auriga Road. The dialogue between the children might run like this:

*Emily*: Shall we go across the park? We could meet my sister when she comes out of school.

*Aisha*: OK. I imagine a gate that you can push open to get into the park.

*Emily*: Yes, it's a wooden gate. There's a metal latch.

*Aisha*: And that kind of metal fencing at each side, you know the sort of diamond shape.

*Teacher*: Chain-link fencing?

*Aisha*: Yes. And there are conker trees just across the path.

*Emily*: Let's go and pick up some conkers. There are lots on the ground . . .

*Teacher*: Notice that at this time of year there will be plenty of fallen leaves. Notice their colours . . .

*Emily*: Reds and yellows.

*Aisha*: I picked up some leaves and some of them are crispy and dry, but others are kind of damp.

*Teacher*: Smell the leaves. [Notice the children's facial expressions and whether their hands actually come up to their faces.] What words can you use to help me to smell those leaves too?

And so it continues. If you choose to guide the visualisation, do so with a light touch – just enough to help the children to get a multi-sensory experience out of the activity.

*Tip*: When the children are more experienced at doing visualisations they can enjoy stories more deeply. As you read a story to the class, pause from time to time and ask children what they are thinking about – what scene they imagine, what colours they envisage, what sounds they hear, what smells and textures they can experience now. The increased richness of these imagined sensory details will be of benefit in their creative and descriptive writing too.

## SENSORY JOURNEY CARD GAME

Creating a pack of sensory cards helps to enrich children's visualisations. On each card place a single word or short phrase. For example, 'colours', 'pick up', 'notice smell', 'go right', 'look from a bird's-eye view'. Use the cards to introduce variety to your whole-group visualisations: children working in pairs can find them useful too if they run short of ideas.

*Note*: Developing children's ability to visualise means that they can experience factual material more powerfully. If you are doing a lesson on dinosaurs, for example, have the children take that imaginative leap back into the world of the dinosaurs. Notice colours, sounds, smells and textures. Any visual material you show them, such as TV programmes, will help of course, although technology won't give the children the smells and textures, not yet anyway!

*Sources*:

Day, J. *Creative Visualization with Children*, Shaftsbury, Dorset: Element, 1994.
Hall, C., Hall, E. and Leech, A. *Scripted Fantasy in the Classroom*, London: Routledge, 1994.

## SOUND FX

This simple game develops auditory awareness and metacognition. Write onomatopoeic words ('noise words' that imitate the sounds they name) on a series of flash cards or as PowerPoint slides. A substantial number of cards will be needed. Use them with the children in these various ways:

- Hold up cards one at a time and ask the children what sounds the words make. Then ask the children to notice what thoughts they had as they read a given card. Note that these might be memories, visual images, auditory impressions (hearing the sounds mentally), kinaesthetic impressions (e.g. the mental feel of water as they read 'gurgle'). Many children may experience a mixture of sensory modalities. Also ask the children to notice if their thoughts were 'large, overview' type impressions or 'small-scale, detailed' impressions. This activity will familiarise the children with their preferred ways of thinking and give practice in exploring other sensory modes.

- Shuffle the cards and give some out to each child or working group. Ask the children to lay the cards out in a line. Suggest that a story is happening here. What is the plot? What other sounds would occur between the ones on the cards that would add more detail to the narrative?

- Give out sets of cards to each working group and have the children separate them out into different categories of sound – liquid sounds, metallic sounds, hard sounds, soft sounds and loud sounds.

- Add a more kinaesthetic element by asking the children to use everyday objects to make sounds – a spoon being dropped into an empty coffee mug, for example. Ask the children to write the sound down, pointing out that what's important is the consideration they give to choosing for themselves how the word could be spelt (with the understanding that various spellings are acceptable). When the children have done this, compare their onomatopoeic words with the actual sounds. Look also at whether standard responses such as 'clatter' or 'tinkle' accurately reflect the sound itself.

- Explore complex or multilayered sounds. Let the children listen to the sound of the ocean, for instance. Encourage them to realise that it is not one sound but a subtle blending of many sounds. How could those sounds be described in more detail?

- Sound effects stories. Help the children to make up simple storylines where the plot is conveyed mainly by sounds, with minimal dialogue. If you have the time, let the children record their 'SFX' tales. Play them back to another group and ask those children what they thought was happening.

- Listening to voices. Listen to various examples of the human voice and explore its many qualities. You might start by asking the children to notice these aspects:

  o Volume: loud – quiet
  o Tone: bass – treble
  o Pitch: high – low
  o Tempo: fast – slow
  o Distance: close – far
  o Rhythm: rhythmic – arrhythmic.

Encourage the children to notice how these aspects change depending upon the emotion being expressed. Listen to speeches by charismatic/persuasive speakers. How do they use the voice to help achieve such a powerful effect, irrespective of the content?

Note that when children are more familiar with these different vocal qualities they are more likely to exercise greater control when reading aloud.

## WHAT COLOUR IS THIS MUSIC?

Usually we describe colours in visual terms and music in musical (auditory) terms. In fact, our language is rich in words that aid all of our senses. But what if we pretended that a musical note had a colour? Imagine hearing the *peep* of a penny whistle. If it had a colour, what colour would it be? Or what about the deep bass notes of a trombone?

I don't know what went on in your mind just then, but I imagined the penny whistle making a sparkly silver note, while the trombone tones were amber-coloured, tending to brown. I can do a sound-to-colour crossover quite easily. Maybe your mind works differently, so instead let's pretend something else. If sandpaper had a smell and/or taste, what would it be? I imagined a harsh bitter coffee taste, but I wasn't as sure of this as of the silver sound of the penny whistle. Maybe you do texture-to-taste crossovers better than I do.

Crossmatching the senses in this way is part of something our brains do called 'synaesthesia'. Some people (the books tell us about 4 per cent) experience crossovers so vividly that it seems utterly real, sometimes to the point of hallucination. Most people, however, make crossovers in their imagination.

Playing synaesthesia games helps children to develop their imagination and also allows them to use the vocabulary they have in richer and more varied ways. Here are some ideas:

- Play a piece of instrumental music and say to the children, 'Pretend this music is a person. As you listen, write down or remember what you notice about your person.'

*Tip 1*: Use the word notice rather than see, as it is a more neutral word that can apply to all of the senses.

*Tip 2*: If a child says 'I can't do this', you can say 'Pretend you can and tell me when you've done it.' This usually gets the result you want.

- Show your group a piece of abstract art and say 'Pretend this picture is a tune. What musical instruments or notes do you hear?'
- Have the children bring in pieces of material, tin foil, pebbles, leaves, and other small objects. Put the children into pairs. One child closes his eyes. The other child holds an object and says 'When you hold this object, pretend it is a sound and tell me what sound you imagine.'
- Take a feeling such as happiness. Say 'If happiness had a shape what shape would it be?'

*Tip*: You can extend this activity by pointing out to children that we often link colours with moods and feelings. What colour is anger, for example? Get children to find others: someone can be green with envy, or feeling blue. These are traditional links. It's fine for a child to say 'When I feel envy it's bright orange!'

Develop the idea by giving feelings not just a colour but a sound, a shape, a texture, etc. This builds into a strategy for helping children to describe their feelings. Also, if they change the colours, sounds, etc. of feelings in their imagination, they can also change the feeling itself as they experience it. This is a good technique to teach in Personal, Social and Health Education (PSHE).

*Another tip*: Get the children to look back at creative writing they've done recently. Very often visual thinkers will use mainly visual descriptions, while kinaesthetic children will tend to talk more about the shapes and sizes of things and characters' feelings. Have the children make notes in the margin about sensory impressions they've left out. If a child has done a visual description of a place, encourage him to imagine the sounds and smells of that place too.

Encourage the children to do multisensory writing from then on. Build in sensory crossovers to make their descriptions more original. If a character in a story smells fresh bread, ask the author to think about the colour of that smell, its sound, etc. You'll get some startling results.

## PERCEPTUAL FILTERING

We see the world not as it really is but as we imagine it to be. Our perceptions are influenced by our own first-hand experiences of course, but also by what others say and what we see on TV and read in the newspapers. In other words, our reality is 'filtered' in all sorts of ways to create the impression we have of the world and of ourselves.

There are many important implications arising from this idea. One is that we can use the power of our creative imaginations to realise that our view of the world is subjective. 'Realise' in this sense means to 'make real' in our thoughts, feelings and actions. As teachers we can presuppose that our children have great imaginations and the potential to think effectively. Our expectations of this will influence the children in a deep and positive way (see Rosenthal, R. *Pygmalion in the Classroom: Teacher Expectation and Pupils' Intellectual Development* [1968, expanded edition 1992] for some startling research on this topic).

Children's creativity develops more quickly in the right environment. Some tips for establishing the creative classroom are:

- Failures of capability in children are often caused by failures of nerve and failures of imagination. That is to say that children's abilities are often held back when they are frightened of having a go and being wrong, and when they can't, won't or don't imagine themselves succeeding. Developing creativity usually boosts self-confidence and this diminishes the influence of failures of imagination and nerve.

- Also help children to lose these failures by using quick feedback and sincere praise. When you ask children to carry out a thinking task, verify clearly and promptly that they have done the mental behaviour you want. Sincerely value the outcomes of the thinking. Even if an answer is wrong we can credit the mental work that the child has done.
- Remember though that often creative thinking is not about right or wrong answers, but generating lots of ideas and then reflecting on them to increase their usefulness.
- Help children to see themselves as great thinkers by encouraging observational skill, metacognition (noticing and modifying one's own thoughts) and a willingness to question.
- Use children's own imaginations as a resource to make them realise that they are all highly creative.

Play the 'eye-view' game. Show the children a photograph of, say, an ordinary street. Say 'Pretend you can step into that picture and, when you do, you are a burglar. What thoughts and feelings come to you now?' At a later date, using the same picture, have the children pretend they are old people living alone.

An interesting and often amusing variation is to have the children pretend they are aliens visiting Earth for the first time. They do not know words like 'houses' or 'cars' or 'people'. Encourage them to think of other descriptions for these. In one workshop a boy imagined people as 'little sticks with hairy tufts on top and bits of cloth hanging from them'. A cat was a 'fuzzy blob of nosiness' and a motorbike became 'a noisy bad-tempered robot always breaking wind'.

Play 'What colour is this feeling?' Refer to 'What colour is this music?', above. As a child imagines the colour, have him dim it down if you are working with a negative feeling and brighten it up if you are working with a positive one.

Combine these ideas to help children see people differently. If child A 'looks down' on child B, have A increase B's size in his mind. If feelings accompany the original perception, work with child A to modify them in a positive way.

If child C is frightened of doing badly in a test, have her imagine that fear of failure as a person. When she has described the person, help her to change it. Give the personification a Donald Duck voice, make it smaller or give it funny clothes.

In short, use your own creativity to help your children use theirs.

## NOTE

1 See my book *Developing Literacy and Creative Writing Through Storymaking* in the Bibliography.

## CHAPTER 2
# Jumpstart creative questioning

Quality questioning is a key component of developing children's creativity and thinking. There are 'routine questions' and there are 'quality questions'. Here are a few common routine classroom questions:

- How many times have I told you to keep the noise down?
- Shall I put my book away now Miss?
- Shall I do this in pencil or pen?
- Now, do you remember what I told you last lesson?
- Can I go to the toilet Sir?
- What is the objective of this lesson?

Some routine questions simply lubricate the day-to-day machinery of the classroom and are necessary on that level. Others limit thinking to the point where we as teachers are merely asking children to recall a fact we have told them earlier. Also, as adults we might use rhetorical questions as a subtle but shallow way of imposing and maintaining our authority – 'Do you expect me to wait all day for you to be quiet?' Routine questions applied to knowledge cause children to use routine kinds of thinking to answer them – either simple recall of that knowledge or recourse to mechanically learned techniques, which are often used without much deep understanding.

Quality questions, on the other hand, open up thinking by giving children more ways of handling ideas. This allows knowledge to become information supported by understanding, by the child's ownership of ideas and by an increasing sense of authority in discussing those ideas. Once children realise that many kinds of questions exist, and are unafraid of asking questions, they have grasped the basic principles of quality questioning.

## OPEN OR CLOSED?

What is the difference between these questions?

- What time is lunch?
- How might we solve the problem of famine in Africa?

Both are to do with food, but the first question presupposes one answer that is satisfied by a single piece of information. It is a small-scale, routine closed question. Represent it to children by using this shape > because it narrows down to a point (convergent thinking). The second question is large-scale, open, and invites many answers arising out of further questions, discussion and the use of creative strategies for solution. Represent it to children like this < (divergent thinking).

Begin developing the children's ability to ask quality questions by encouraging them to make distinctions about the questions they ask and encounter. 'Audit' your own questions to make sure you ask plenty of open questions that stimulate the use of creative thinking techniques.

A simple activity for encouraging the asking of closed questions is to show the children a picture of a house and suggest that there is a person inside, but you don't know what he or she looks like. Have the children ask closed questions – 'Is the person female?' 'Is the person tall?', etc. Flip a coin to find an answer: heads = yes; tails = no. The children learn to build subsequent questions upon the information gleaned by previous answers.

Note also that the 'Twenty questions' game (page 49) also helps to develop clear and unambiguous closed questioning.

## 'ANSWER QUESTIONS' OR 'QUESTION QUESTIONS'?

Another important distinction between types of questions is whether they lead to definite answers or are designed to generate more questions. The first kind are termed scientific/technical questions (this is a generic term and doesn't apply only to science and technology). Questions of this sort presuppose that the answers exist 'out there' in the world and can be found by investigation. Scientific questions can be small-scale and routine ('What is the capital city of England?') or large-scale, open and creative ('How did the Earth form?'). Although scientific-type questions are often divergent ultimately, reaching the answers often demands exploration across many areas of knowledge.

The second kind, 'question questions', are also called philosophical questions. They tend to be asked to stimulate discussion of deep themes, the meanings of words and ideas, and the nature of thought and reality. These questions don't necessarily presuppose that any final and definitive answers exist. The learning is in the thinking/talking rather than in coming to definite decisions. Themes that are often explored through philosophical questions and discussion are:

- Life and death
- The nature of reality
- Consciousness and thought
- Morality, guilt, justice
- The nature and meaning of beliefs
- God.

Stimulate children's thinking and discussion by asking questions around these themes. Very often 'What if . . . ?' questions do the trick. Try these:

- What if you had a stopwatch that could stop time (but you could still keep moving around)?
- What if you could swap bodies with another person?
- What if you had a time machine?
- What if we could all read each other's thoughts?
- What if speaking didn't exist?
- What if you had three wishes?

If you want to find out more about discussing philosophical issues with your children, Stephen Law's *Philosophy Files* books are a great introduction (see references on page 16).

An increasing number of schools are developing P4C (Philosophy for Children) into their curriculum. A teaching pack for achieving this is *But Why?* (see reference on page 16).

# A QUESTION A DAY

We are used to setting time aside for literacy, numeracy, topic work, etc. Quality questioning is basic to children's development in all of these and many more areas. Build questioning behaviour into all that you do in class. Here are a few springboard suggestions:

## Questions noticeboard

Dedicate one display space on your wall to the exploration of questions. Jumpstart the process by pinning a question on the board and inviting children to write possible answers on cards which are then pinned around it. The answers might be factual or opinions supported by reasoning. 'Which is the best football team in the country?' is the kind of question to encourage opinion and reasoning type answers. 'How can we stop graffiti?' encourages creative thinking.

## What happened?

Create a scenario and invite the children to come up with explanations that account for most or all of the observed evidence. So, for instance:

- The downstairs lounge window of the Jones's house has been forced open.
- There are no footprints in the flower border just outside the lounge window.
- Half the block of ice-cream in the freezer has been eaten.
- The family dog did not bark.
- There is a single washed dessert spoon in the cutlery holder on the kitchen sink.
- Mr Jones's best suit is missing from the wardrobe in the bedroom.
- There is a box of chocolates on the bed.
- There is a pen and a memo pad on the lounge table.
- There is no note on the lounge table.

Invite the children to come up with their explanations. Encourage weird and wonderful scenarios as much as mundane ones. Do not allow children to ask questions while they formulate their ideas.

Because I made up the scenario above I have my own idea of what went on. Mr Jones came home but needed to go out again to an important formal meeting. He discovered he had misplaced his house keys so needed to break in. He forced the lounge window because this was the least inconvenient. He is a keen gardener and so took care not to disturb his flowerbed. The family dog, recognising his master, did not bark at him. Mr Jones had brought his wife a box of chocolates and left them on the bed as he changed into his business suit. He didn't have time to eat a proper tea, so hurriedly wolfed down some ice-cream before leaving. Because he is a tidy man he washed up his spoon. He scribbled a brief note to his wife and left it on the lounge table, but as he rushed out the draught blew the note off the table . . .

Now that you know what I think happened you can invite the children to ask questions to elicit further information – make it up, as long as it's consistent with the story. Focus their attention by saying something like 'Ask some things about the Jones family.' With more information available, the children will be able to work out your version of events.

When the children are familiar with the 'What happened?' game, help them to write their own scenarios.

## TWENTY QUESTIONS

This is a perennially popular game that can be used to develop children's quality questioning behaviour. I suggest you establish these rules before starting:

- Think about the question before asking it.
- Base your question (except for the first few questions) on what you have already learned.
- No wild guesses are allowed. You can say what you think the chosen word is if you give reasons for your choice.

Try these variations on the game:

- Parts of speech 'Twenty questions'. Display a number of words covering different parts of speech. For each part of speech include variations – so make sure you have verbs of different tenses and a selection of nouns (abstract, concrete and proper). Build in comparison of adjectives by including 'bigger', 'best', 'most beautiful', etc. Encourage children to use the vocabulary of grammar as they narrow down the options.
- Where am I? This is a good way of exploring coordinates and map symbols. Use a detailed map and pick a spot. This is where you are 'hiding'. The class can ask up to 20 questions to try and discover where you are. Again, encourage the children to use geographical vocabulary in their questions.
- Timelines. Use historical timelines featuring significant dates, events, characters. Choose a year and challenge the children to find out where on the timeline you are hiding. Don't settle for too many 'Is it before 1066?/Is it after 1945?' type questions: encourage the children to use the dates, events and characters on the timeline as part of their vocabulary of questioning.
- Gridwork. Use a grid such as the example in Figure 2.1, opposite. Around the grid display some of the vocabulary you want the children to use in formulating their questions – mammal, live young, fly, wings, domestic, extinct, faster, predator, etc.

*Tip 1*: Create a sense of 'beating your personal best'. If the class come to the right answer in 15 questions, next time ask the children if they can do it in 14 questions – or maybe less!

*Tip 2*: Question analysis. On some occasions at least it's worth recording the children's questions for further analysis. Look at whether questions are open or closed, large-scale or small-scale; how much understanding seems to lie behind them, how far any question narrows down the options, etc. This kind of looking back will help children to formulate more incisive and powerful questions subsequently.

**Figure 2.1:** Twenty questions

## QUESTION HOOKS

Turn a question mark upside down and it becomes a hook – on which to hang more questions, and on which to catch the interest of young learners. Use this idea to make the following:

- Question mobile. This might consist of a big open question on which are hung subsidiary questions. The structure of the mobile can be designed beforehand, but if time is short and an actual 3D mobile is not practical, the technique works just as well as a 'question pyramid' on paper, as in Figure 2.2 on page 53.
- Question tree. Again, this idea can be made more tactile by using an artificial Christmas tree or any small sapling outside. You might want the children to cut out paper leaves on which to write their questions. Alternatively the idea makes a striking

wall display. The branching structure of the tree is especially apt to demonstrate that some questions have multiple answers and can give rise to many further questions. The tree metaphor also suggests that all questions have their roots in the soil of natural curiosity and grow 'organically' as we enquire, experiment, investigate and learn more.

## QUESTION STAR

Six key question words are: where, when, what, who, how, why? Arrange these around a six-pointed star to create a visual organiser for systematically asking questions. Visual organisers are powerful because, although we have a conscious tendency to think in visual, auditory and kinaesthetic ways (or usually blends of these), most of the information that becomes encoded in the brain enters through the eyes. Visually organised material tends to be remembered more easily and more completely.

The question star also provides a springboard for the introduction or revisiting of mind mapping. This technique is powerful partly because it is highly visual, but also because the information is 'holistic' – everything is available at a glance – and because links can immediately be seen between different ideas in the network. Here are four important elements for mind mapping:

1. Different categories of information are organised in different parts of the visual field.
2. The categories are colour coded for easy visual access.
3. Key words form 'nuclei' around which further ideas can be clustered.
4. The organisation builds a network of ideas, but further links can also be made between visually widely separated ideas. In other words a deliberate mental connection is forged: knowledge becomes more truly information – 'in-formation', the formation of greater meanings and understandings and more complex ideas.

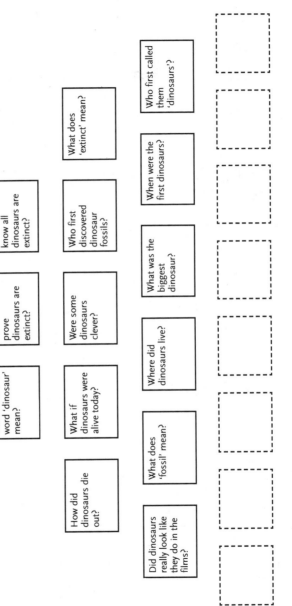

**Figure 2.2:** Question pyramid

Dinosaurs became extinct 65 million years ago.

How can we prove dinosaurs are extinct?

How do we know all dinosaurs are extinct?

What does the word 'dinosaur' mean?

What if dinosaurs were alive today?

Were some dinosaurs clever?

Who first discovered dinosaur fossils?

What does 'extinct' mean?

How did dinosaurs die out?

What does 'fossil' mean?

Where did dinosaurs live?

What was the biggest dinosaur?

When were the first dinosaurs?

Who first called them 'dinosaurs'?

Did dinosaurs really look like they do in the films?

Create a kinaesthetic mind map. Place a six-pointed star in the centre of a table. On each of six cards write the key question words, using a different colour for each. Having decided on your topic or piece of jumpstart information (e.g. 'Dinosaurs became extinct 65 million years ago'), write this on a card and place it in the middle of the star. Now encourage the children to write further questions on more cards – using the agreed colours – and place them in the appropriate areas of the map. Here are some refinements of the technique:

- Help the children to review the mapped questions. If two or more questions are similar, physically overlap the cards (or write them out again in a Venn diagram to reflect the links yet also the differences between the questions).
- Number the cards before you give them out to the children (so that every question has a number later). Write the numbers on small scraps of paper, put them in a bag and do a lucky dip. When children pick out a number they find the corresponding question and can then either think of further subsidiary questions and/or research possible answers.
- Take any one of the questions from the map and use it as the jumpstart question for another question and/or answer mind map. So if we chose 'Who first discovered dinosaur fossils?', this would be placed in the middle of a question star. It might stimulate further questions, such as:

  o Where and when were the first fossils found?
  o What did people think they were?
  o Do people disagree about who found the first fossils?
  o Were the first fossils discovered by accident?
  o Do those first fossils still exist in museums? (Where? Are they valuable?)
  o Can other things apart from dinosaurs turn into fossils?
  o Are there things that cannot be fossilised?

*Source*: Buzan, T. *Use Your Head*, London: BBC Books, 1993.

## QUESTION WEB

I also call this a 'cloud of questions'. Children's learning is limited when they are merely the passive recipients of facts within a content-led curriculum. The ability to retain and reiterate knowledge is not always a very sure indicator of understanding or personal 'ownership' of information (where children make ideas their own to the extent that they can express them in a variety of ways, and link them with other concepts). Encouraging children actively to question the knowledge they encounter develops understanding and helps creative thinking more generally.

A question web is simply a visual mapping of questions surrounding a chosen idea, and how those questions lead to further questions (although it need not strictly reflect the organisational principles of a Buzan-style mind map).

Begin by placing an idea in the middle of a large noticeboard or a tabletop (if you can spare the space!). For example, 'The Sun lies at the centre of our Solar System'. This is a simple and commonly known fact but it still begs many questions. Why does the Sun lie at the centre? What is a 'sun'? Why is it called the 'Solar System'? What is a system? What does the word 'solar' mean? And so on. As children come up with these questions, write them out on pieces of paper and stick the pieces around the central idea.

Encourage the children now either to research the answers to one or more of the questions, or to think of further questions. When an answer is found, stick it beside its corresponding question. What other questions now occur? Answer: The Sun lies at the centre of the Solar System because of its great size and gravitational pull, which keeps the planets and other objects in orbit around it. Further questions: What does 'gravitational pull' mean? Can something that isn't of great size have a gravitational pull? Is the word 'orbit' linked with 'orb'? What is a planet? What other objects go around the Sun? And so on.

Gradually a 'cloud' of questions will come to surround the original concept. The educational value of this activity is:

- It shifts the emphasis away from children receiving facts passively to actively questioning them and searching for meaningful answers.
- It feels 'safer' to ask questions when that is the focus of the activity and the behaviour that is being sought and praised by the teacher. (Consider the difference between the teacher saying 'Well done, Thomas, you've asked ten questions today' and 'Thomas, you didn't know the answers to any of those ten questions today'.) The implication behind the activity is that what's important isn't 'not knowing' but wanting to find out. This reflects the development of human understanding itself, from a position of greater ignorance to one of less ignorance.
- The visual aspect of the question web helps to make meaningful links between ideas, whether they are in the form of questions or answers. The notion of the interconnectedness of knowledge is made more explicit now.
- The 'Question web' activity often takes you, the teacher, beyond your own 'comfort zone' of already knowing the answers. An old piece of wisdom advises us that a good teacher is never afraid to say 'I don't know, but how can we find out?' Learning is surely more about the process of searching for truth (as far as we can find it) than just accepting facts.
- The activity can easily be extended into the realm of 'meta questioning' with children who increasingly feel comfortable as questioning learners. Meta questioning uses questions to investigate questions. Which of these is the more difficult question to answer and why – 'What is gravity?', 'Why does the Sun shine?', 'How old are you?' Why do some questions have lots of answers but some seem just to have one definite right answer? Does the word 'right' in the phrase 'right answer' always mean the same thing? Can an answer be 'right' for one person and 'wrong' for another? If this is true, can we ever have completely 'right' answers to questions like these? If I could ask [choose a person] three important questions, what would they be?

## A MATTER OF FACT

The word 'fact' can be traced back to the Latin *facere*, 'to make'. It has a link with 'manufacture', which originally meant 'to make by hand'. I think this is important because it helps us to realise that facts are the products of human minds. They are as much the outcomes of thinking as tables and chairs. And they are just as 'real' insofar as we shape them to reflect our perceptions of the world. Also, of course, facts can and do change. Some areas of knowledge and understanding are developing so quickly that what was written about them in last year's encyclopaedias is already out of date.

If we truly want to jumpstart our children's creativity, we must encourage them to question facts and not just accept them passively as 'right answers'. The 'Question star' technique helps in this (see page 52). If we give the class a piece of information – Shakespeare was a great playwright – it is more educationally valuable for children to ask questions than to simply write the idea in their books:

- What does 'great' mean?
- Does everybody think Shakespeare is great?
- Are some of his plays greater than others? Who says so? Why?
- What does 'wright' mean in the word 'playwright'?
- Why is it called a play?

For older children and/or more sophisticated questioners, invite them to ask these questions when they are presented with new information:

- How recent is the information?
- Is the author's information reliable? Does it agree with other information from other sources?
- What is the author's purpose? (To entertain/inform/persuade?)
- How (in some detail) does (s)he do that?
- Does the author have a point of view?

- How does the author use information to support that point of view?
- Is the author biased?
- How is the information presented? How does the presentation contribute to your understanding? (How else could you present the information?)
- Is the presentation logical? Does the author support generalisations?

## A MEDLEY OF QUESTION GAMES

- Question chain. Start with a piece of information. Ask a question about it. Find at least one answer to it. Out of that answer, think of another question. Answer that second question. Out of the answer find a third question – and so on. *'Dinosaurs became extinct 65 million years ago' – What does the word 'dinosaur' mean? – It means 'terrible lizard' – Why do (or did) people think dinosaurs were lizards? – Because some scientists thought they were cold-blooded like lizards still are today – Do all scientists think that dinosaurs were cold-blooded? – No, some scientists like Robert Bakker think some dinosaurs were warm-blooded like mammals – Why does he think this?* In one school I visited we made a question chain using paper links that stretched around all four walls of the classroom and out through the door!
- Directory enquiries. Split the class into two groups. One group are questioners and the other group are researchers/answerers. This second group can have access to books and the internet. The first group generates a number of questions on a chosen topic and the research group has to try and find some possible answers. This will stimulate further questions, which in their turn need to be researched. After a certain time the groups change places.
- Question blog. If you have a school 'intranet' you can set up one or more blogs (web logs). Jumpstart the correspondence with a statement/question/opinion and invite the children to add their comments and further questions. The game can be used to practise information and communications technology (ICT) skills. Hyperlinks to online encyclopaedias help children to research and verify their ideas.

- Question balloons. You will need some helium-filled balloons. Ask each child in the class to write on a card a question that he thinks is important and would really like to know the answer to. On the other side of the card put a brief explanation of the project and that you, as the teacher, would very much appreciate the finder of the card supplying an answer. Add an email address. Now launch the balloons and wait to see what answers come back.

## QUESTION QUOTES

Put aphorisms (short statements of truth or opinion) that highlight the value of questions and questioning around the classroom. Here are some of my favourites:

> Everything must be laid bare – All of the dark and hidden secrets of the world.
>
> (Leonardo da Vinci)

> I think, at a child's birth, if a mother could ask a fairy god-mother to endow it with the most useful gift, that gift would be curiosity.
>
> (Eleanor Roosevelt [1884–1962], American diplomat, writer, US First Lady)

> Curiosity is one of the most permanent and certain characteristics of a vigorous mind.
>
> (Samuel Johnson)

> The important thing is not to stop questioning.
>
> (Albert Einstein)

> You can tell whether someone is clever by his answers. You can tell whether someone is wise by his questions.
>
> (Ancient Proverb)

> I'm not a teacher, only a fellow traveller of whom you asked the way. I pointed ahead – ahead of myself as well as of you.
>
> (George Bernard Shaw)

59

# CHAPTER 3

# Jumpstart creative reasoning

Creativity is sometimes believed to be a rather chaotic process where inspiration, if you are lucky, might strike from 'out of the blue' and can thus be quite haphazard and time-consuming. If this were the case, then it would be difficult to cater for the development of creativity in schools: special provision would have to be made for the needs of the eccentric minority who may indeed grow up to be geniuses, if only they were connected to the real world . . .

Luckily we are all creative in the sense that we can think things that we have never connected before in our minds and have the ability to look at ideas in many ways. We also have an inbuilt curiosity – we are all naturally nosy. These predispositions depend as much upon conscious reasoning as they do upon the subconscious processing that gives rise to 'Eureka' moments of sudden insight. Furthermore, creative thinking in that sense can be applied to any area of knowledge. In my opinion it underpins even what we recognise as core skills such as numeracy and literacy. If it lies at the heart of education, it is a powerful engine that drives all areas of learning.

## CREATIVE CUT UPS

This is a simple technique with wide application. Information that has already been put into a sequence is scrambled. The task is to re-sequence it in a reasoned order. A basic 'cut ups' task would be to write the surnames of all the children in the class on separate scraps of paper and have the children arrange the names into alphabetical order. You will, I'm sure, be able to think of many variations of this kind of game.

The value of cut ups is that children can physically arrange and rearrange the information until they are satisfied. They are not 'committing' themselves to paper. Cut ups games also generate much discussion. And if you take the trouble to print the information pieces on card and then laminate them, you have created a durable resource.

Here are a few ideas for more challenging cut ups games:

### Out of this world

Take a more complex sequence, such as the order of the planets outward from the Sun. Present the information in a more subtle way than simply saying 'Mercury is the first planet, Venus is the second planet' etc. The result could look like this:

- Neptune lies beyond Uranus.
- Mercury circles the Sun inside the orbit of the Earth.
- Neptune is the eighth planet of nine (if we still regard Pluto as a planet).
- Venus orbits the Sun between Earth and Mercury.
- Mars is next outward from the Sun after Earth.
- Jupiter and Saturn both orbit closer to the Sun than Uranus does.
- Jupiter orbits farther from the Sun than Mars.
- Saturn is the seventh planet outward from the Sun.
- Mercury orbits closest to the Sun.

You will see immediately that more reasoning is called for here than just putting the planets in 'numerical order' outward from the Sun. Extend the game by asking children to make up different statements that would allow another group to recreate the sequence of planets.

### A day in the life of Mr Squibbs

Create some information about how Mr Squibbs spent his day and ask the children to recreate a timeline:

- Mr Squibbs went to bed at 9.30 p.m.
- After breakfast Mr Squibbs went to the shopping centre.
- Mr Squibbs ate lunch after he had visited his friend Mr Wint.
- Mr Wint phoned Mr Squibbs at 10.15 a.m. and invited him round for a coffee.

Once children are familiar with the way the information scraps are sequenced they can create their own – either for a completely new timeline, or to add to what we already know about Mr Squibbs' day.

## Discussion and debate

Choose a topic to be debated and assemble ideas that argue for and against the case. These might be facts, reasons, opinions, assumptions, etc. and will be of greater or lesser significance to the point. The example I've chosen is 'Should car parking charges be introduced by the Town Council?' In this case some of the cut ups could be:

- Car parking charges encourage people to use public transport.
- Philippa Stephens prefers using her car for reasons of personal safety.
- Ben Leech is on a low income. He works in the town and won't be able to afford to park his car there if charges are introduced.
- Traffic flow through the town has increased by 50 per cent over the past five years.
- The government has cut the money it gives to the Town Council by 7 per cent this year.
- If car parking charges happen, people won't use the shops in town. Instead they'll go to the out-of-town shopping centre where parking is free.
- We should all use cars less because of global warming.
- Bus services to villages outside town are very poor.

The task for the children is to arrange the pieces of information into two groups – For and Against the idea of car parking charges. Then they refine their arrangement into facts and opinions and/or the relative importance of the ideas to the argument. One benefit of this version of the cut ups game is that the children themselves can research the topic and add further information to the stock of cut ups. Educationally the game is beneficial because all of the children are exposed to both sides of the issue in detail.

*Tip*: This kind of cut ups game can be used with the 'Decision alley' technique on page 97.

### Philosophical and moral issues

The cut ups activity in this case follows the pattern of the car parking game above, but now there is more focus on things like generalisations, emotive language, interpretation of particular words, valid or invalid arguments, etc. The children's task is to build a case for or against by using the most powerful ideas. As an example let's use the proposition that 'It is morally wrong to eat meat'. Some of the scraps (of paper, not meat) could be:

- It is better to kill an older animal for meat than a younger animal because the older animal has already lived out most of its life.
- What if a human being had a brain injury and didn't know right from wrong? Would it be wrong then if (s)he killed an animal for food?
- All animals have the right to life.
- All animals have the right to live out their natural life span.
- All animals have the right to live out their natural lifespan peacefully.
- Our bodies are built to eat meat as well as vegetables (we are omnivores), so therefore it's natural for us to want to eat meat.
- It's my life and I can do what I want.
- What does 'morally' mean? Do we decide what is morally right and wrong, or does God (whatever 'God' means) decide for us?
- Animals eat other animals. Are they morally wrong?
- If a tribe of people could avoid starving to death only by killing and eating animals, would they be wrong to do so?

You and/or the children themselves can add further ideas. Stephen Law's excellent *Philosophy Files* books (see references on page 16) will give you plenty of ideas for information scraps on this and other issues. I also recommend Cohen, M. *101 Ethical Dilemmas*, London: Routledge, 2003.

## PREDICTION STRIPS

This is an extension of the cut ups activity above. Information can be written out on strips of paper to add a kinaesthetic element and make the activity more adaptable. In its simplest version it resembles the old logic exercise of 'What comes next?' – A-B-C-D-? or A-?-C-?-E or 1-2-3-4-?. This in itself is a versatile technique which can be focussed into any subject area and pitched at any level of difficulty and challenge.

To make it a more creative exercise, try these variations:

Show the children part of a sequence and have them work out what comes next and what comes before: ?-?-?-D-E-F-?-?-?. Or have a longer strip with several gaps in the sequence, which makes the game more challenging.

Create two parallel prediction strips and ask children to make logical connections between them. This can take the pattern 'If . . . then . . . because . . .' So 'If Z = 26, then A = 1 because . . .' Or you might phrase it 'Z is to 26 as A is to 1 because . . .' This is one of the classic patterns of *analogy*. The word comes from the Greek and means a correspondence or proportion. Originally it referred to a mathematical proportion, but the idea can be used more generally. Below are some other analogy patterns with ideas for using them with prediction strips.

- Cause to effect. Make up a simple table like this:

| Cause | One effect | Another effect |
|---|---|---|
| The glass falls | The glass . . . ? | |
| A ball is kicked | The ball . . . ? | Or the ball . . . ? |
| The air in the balloon is . . . ? | The balloon rises | |
| Success results – | – in . . . ? | Or in . . . ? |
| . . . ? results – | – in misery | Or in . . . ? |

*Tip*: Point out to children that not all of these puzzles have just one right answer. Encourage children to use the word 'because' in explaining their reasons or opinions.

- Create two (or more) parallel strips where only parts of each sequence match up. Children have to position the strips so that the matching sequences correspond.
- Another kind of analogy is a word and its synonym. Using this pattern the strips would look like this:

| Big | Tall | Happy | Sad | Leave | Bad | Eager | Brave |
|-----|------|-------|-----|-------|-----|-------|-------|
| Old | Strong | Glad | Unhappy | Depart | Late | Busy | Fearless |

- Use the same arrangement for synonym–antonym, numbers and their multiples, countries and their capital cities, animals and their young, etc. Make the activity more challenging by using three or more strips: word + two antonyms; country + capital + flag; gradations (one – ten – hundred – thousand – million); comparison of adjectives (good – better – best).
- Imagine a prediction strip like a strip of film. Each 'frame' features a sentence or picture. Some frames are left blank and children are asked to interpret what story they tell and then predict which words and/or pictures could fill them (see Figure 3.1 on page 66). Vary the activity as follows:

  o Supply several strips containing words and pictures to complement the main strip. Ask children which strip they'd add to the main one, and why.
  o Put words/pictures into the middle of a story strip, leaving the beginning and the end blank. Ask children to complete the story.

*Tip*: To make the task easier, have two parallel strips. One of them features pictures that help children to fill in the words missing from frames in the second strip.

  o Comic cut ups. Cut out the panels of a comic strip and ask children to put the pieces back into sequence. Or, if there are 20 panels, give the children 15 of them plus 5 blank pieces of paper. As the children sequence the panels ask them to suggest what pictures should go on the blank pieces and why.

## Basic prediction strip:

| Richard was on his way home when he found a purse lying on the pavement. | He looked inside the purse and found the name and address of the owner. | He decided to take the purse round to where the owner lived. On his way he met Sam. | Sam snatched the purse from Richard, took out the money and threw the purse into the hedge. | Richard managed to pull the purse out of the hedge. All the money had gone. What could he do now? | |
|---|---|---|---|---|---|

Or:

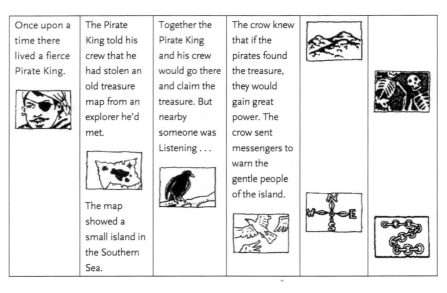

| Once upon a time there lived a fierce Pirate King. | The Pirate King told his crew that he had stolen an old treasure map from an explorer he'd met. The map showed a small island in the Southern Sea. | Together the Pirate King and his crew would go there and claim the treasure. But nearby someone was Listening . . . | The crow knew that if the pirates found the treasure, they would gain great power. The crow sent messengers to warn the gentle people of the island. | | |
|---|---|---|---|---|---|

Or:

**Figure 3.1:** Prediction strips for stories

## STRUCTURE AND FUNCTION

Asking children to offer ideas about how the structure of an object relates to its function sharpens their observational skills and their ability to reason, speculate, infer and reach a conclusion.

As a first example we'll use a wok, wok lid and spatula (because I like to cook stir-fry).

**Figure 3.2:** Wok, wok lid and spatula

Ideally, bring these things into the classroom for children to see and handle for themselves. If this isn't possible use a picture, together with a brief description. Also, show the class a YouTube clip of someone cooking a simple stir-fry dish.

Note that most woks are made of carbon steel or cast iron, while the lids are often very thin aluminium.

Begin by asking the children what they notice about these items. Descriptive points to look for are:

1. The wok is very wide (and is a half sphere).
2. The metal is thin.
3. The wok is round on the bottom (though some have a flattened base so they sit stably on an electric or induction hob).
4. The wok has a long handle that is wooden at the end. (Some woks have two small, looped metal handles.)
5. The spatula is wide and flat, with turned up sides. (Some spatulas are like wide slotted spoons.)
6. The wok lid is thin and light.

And while watching the stir-fry demonstration:

7. The cook heats the wok first so that it is very hot, even smoking a little.
8. The cook swirls the oil so that it covers most of the inside of the wok.
9. The cook keeps the food moving but sometimes leaves it on the sides of the wok (for example, to add a little more oil).
10. The cook stir fries a vegetable like a chopped pepper, then takes the pieces out and sets them aside before adding a softer vegetable like bean sprouts, or chicken that has been marinated.

Now ask the children to explain their observations. Allow them to speculate freely and refrain from jumping in with the 'right answers'.

1. To prevent food from being flipped over the sides during the stir frying.

2. So that heat conducts quickly throughout. The thin metal also reacts quickly to changes in temperature if these are needed during cooking.
3. So that the oil pools in the bottom and so heats up very quickly. The wok shape also allows hot oil to drain back to the bottom, so that morsels of food can be 'rested' on the sides and not absorb too much oil.
4. So that the cook's hand does not get too close to the heat. Wood does not conduct heat well, so the wooden end to the handle serves as extra protection. The long wooden-ended handle of the spatula serves the same purpose. The slots in the spoon allow liquid to drain away from the food as it is lifted out of the wok. Just the right amount of the sauce that remains in the wok can then be poured over the food.
5. This means that all of the food can be kept moving (so that it doesn't burn or lie around in the oil). The turned-up sides make it easier to scoop up the morsels of food and keep them on the spatula.
6. The lid can cover the food and help keep it hot while, for instance, rice or noodles are put out on the plates. (The lid will also keep steam in during the steaming of a dish.)
7. If the wok and oil are not at a high temperature at the outset, the food will not cook quickly and can absorb more oil, so affecting the texture and taste.
8. So that food doesn't stick to the wok and burn.
9. Placing morsels of food on the sides of the wok means that newly added oil can heat up to temperature before the stir-frying continues.
10. The stir-frying method means that vegetables can be cooked quickly yet retain their crunchiness. Harder vegetables like peppers are added first because they take longer to cook. They are removed as softer vegetables like bean sprouts that require less cooking time, are added. In many stir-fry recipes all the vegetables are removed when morsels of meat are added. When this happens the oil cools briefly. If the vegetables are left in they can become sludgy.

The 'Structure and function' activity can be used with literally thousands of objects and things from the natural world. In my experience most children enjoy trying to figure out why a leaf or flower, an animal or a gadget is the shape it is.

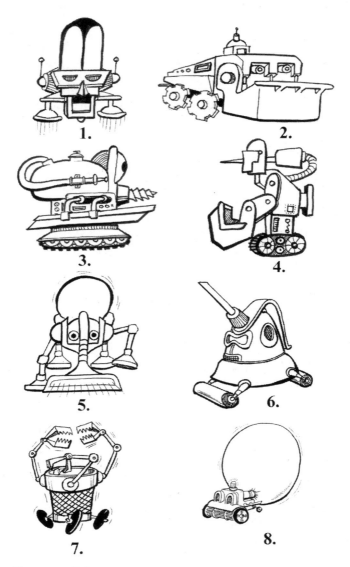

1.

2.

3.

4.

5.

6.

7.

8.

**Figure 3.3:** Robots

*Tip*: Including this activity as part of a topic, in science for example, helps children to retain knowledge more effectively. They are actively engaging with the topic rather than being the passive recipients of abstract facts.

Take it further:

Figure 3.3 shows some robots designed and drawn by artist Tony Hitchman. What do the children think their functions are? Follow up by asking children to design, draw and label a robot of their own.

## ARTIST AND INSTRUCTOR

Choose an object (for example, a house) and write it on a sheet of paper. Choose one child to be the artist. He stands by the board with his drawing implement at the ready. Next choose the instructor. Show the instructor what you have written on the paper. The instructor's job is to describe the object in an 'abstract' way without using the names for things – such as window, door, chimney, wall, etc. As the instructor speaks the artist draws based on what he says. The artist should not ask any questions but simply carry out the instructions based on her best interpretation of them. The child who correctly guesses or works out the answer as the object is drawn can take a turn.

In the example above the instructor might begin:

Draw a large rectangle. Make it as though it was lying on its side. Now you are going to draw four smaller squares inside the rectangle. Go to the top left-hand corner of the rectangle. Place your pen above the very corner. Now move the pen diagonally towards the centre of the rectangle – do it slowly and stop when I tell you . . . OK, stop. Now draw a line downwards until I tell you to stop – stop! Make that the left-hand side of your square. Draw the square . . .

You'll appreciate that the instructor has most of the work to do! This game is not only fun but encourages children to think carefully about what they say. It is also a good way of revisiting the language of geometry.

## THE 'IF . . . THEN . . .' GAME

This game explores cause, effect and consequence in any area of knowledge. It not only tests children's reasoning abilities but is also an effective and enjoyable way of generating ideas for stories. It's a good idea to use if-thens that are wacky and fantastical. This is more fun, although the children still find themselves making valid connections and logical links between ideas as they explore 'real life' issues.

*Tip*: Run the game first as a whole-class oral activity to make children familiar with it. Subsequently different groups of children can be working on different if-thens and record their ideas as sound files or on paper.

As an example we'll take 'If everyone had three wishes, then . . . '. Responses might include:

- Some people would wish for things other people didn't want.
- If that happened, people would have to use a wish to 'wish away' something they didn't want.
- If people knew their wishes would be wasted in that way, they'd talk about what they were going to wish for first.
- If that happened, people would know what lots of other people really wanted.
- If that happened, people would know your deepest thoughts.
- If people were going to know your deepest thoughts, maybe you wouldn't want to tell them.
- If lots of people decided not to tell their deepest thoughts, everyone would find out anyway when you made your wishes.
- If that were going to happen, people would become very clever in disguising their wishes.

At any point you can ask a question, make a suggestion or generally guide the game. For instance, you might say 'What if most people wished for money?'

- If most people wished for money, then there would be too much money in the world.
- If there were that much of it, money would become worthless.
- If clever people knew that, then they wouldn't wish for money. Maybe they'd wish for gold.
- But if that happened, there would be so much gold that gold would become worthless . . .

Notice how the game explores links between power, selfishness, co-operation, wealth, value and other themes.

You can develop the technique by introducing the pattern of 'If . . . then . . . or . . .' This encourages children to come up with more ideas and explore beyond their first thoughts. So if people had three wishes, then they would wish to live longer – or some people might save their wishes and pass them on to their children – or people who already had lots would give their wishes to those whose own wishes hadn't made them happy . . .

## THE 'BECAUSE' GAME

'Because' implies a reason. It is a way of logically linking two or more ideas. When I use the word with children I explain that 'because' is a lovely 'sticky' word: it helps you to stick reasons onto the things you say and believe. Emphasising the word through the '"Because" game' helps children to develop the ability to justify their opinions.

As with the '"If . . . then . . . " game' above, begin with something fantastical. Emphasise that inappropriate responses are not acceptable.

- The dragon was very unhappy . . .
- Because he had lost his fiery breath.
- He had lost his fiery breath because the evil goblin had put a spell on him.
- The evil goblin did that because he was jealous of the dragon.
- He was jealous of the dragon because the dragon was very popular.

- The dragon was popular because he helped lots of people by using his fiery breath. (Here you might ask for examples of how the dragon helped people. Then say:)
- But the goblin couldn't help people because . . . ?

In other words, guide the flow of ideas so that more characters and avenues of exploration are introduced. Again you will see how the '"Because" game' is a quick, enjoyable and effective way of allowing children to generate lots of ideas.

*Tip*: Develop the technique by playing the '"Because . . . maybe . . . or . . . " game'. So – the dragon was unhappy because he had lost his fiery breath. Or maybe because [his best friend had flown away]. Or maybe because [the Chief Dragon had shouted at him]. Or maybe because (his scales were not turning from green to gold like they ought to). This version of the game proceeds by exploring one idea for a while, then backtracking to look at another 'maybe because' and so on. The '"Because . . . maybe . . . or . . . " game' produces so many ideas that it can be difficult to keep track of them. When I run the activity with a class I ask children to draw a tree shape on a large sheet of paper so that we can record all of our ideas.

The '"Because" game' can be made more kinaesthetic in these ways:

- Write each statement in a '"Because" game' onto a strip of paper with the writing on the outer surface. Link these into a 'logic chain'. I have found that groups enjoy competing with each other to see who can produce the longest chain – but as the teacher make sure the children's reasons are adequately 'sticky'.
- 'Because' Post-its. Write out a statement about an issue or theme and attach it to a noticeboard – for example 'Global warming could change our planet in many ways'. Invite children (after they've done some research) to write reasons related to the statement on Post-it notes and stick them to the noticeboard.
- In many schools I've visited the children have drawn pictures of themselves, which have then been put up as a display. Add to this activity by writing beneath each child's picture '[Name] is a valuable member of this class because . . . ?' and ask the other children to consider their classmate's positive qualities, write them on Post-its and stick them around the portrait of that child.

- Character mind map. This is a way of encouraging children to think in detail about characters they can write about in their stories. If you are able to use a visual of the character to be developed, all the better. Put the picture in the centre of the display. Write some statements about the character, positioned appropriately. So 'This character has long, untidy hair.' 'This character has a thin scar on his left cheek.' Invite the children to come up with reasons in the form of 'Maybe because . . .', which are put on Post-its and clustered around the relevant statements.
- Sticky reasons. This can be a simple ten-minute filler. Focus on your topic of enquiry and write a statement – 'Forks have four prongs because . . . ?' Children write possible reasons on Post-its to stick around the statement.
- Reasoning webs. The world is complex and full of uncertainty. Reflect this by combining 'because' with 'but', 'maybe', 'if . . . then . . .', 'therefore' and similar vocabulary of reasoning. Building 'webs of reasoning' onto a wall display creates a visual organiser that will help children to access these involved connections more easily.

Begin by selecting your topic of enquiry. For example, 'Technology has got the world into a mess and it's only technology that can get us out of it'.

Support the children's reasoning in the early stages of creating the web – even to the extent of spoon-feeding them 'answers' if necessary:

- o If technology got the world into a mess, then only more advanced technology can help, because more advanced technology will be less polluting and dangerous.
- o But 'technology' doesn't exist by itself. It's people that create technology, so therefore it's people we need to change to get the world out of the mess it's in.
- o What kind of mess are we talking about? If we talk about 'being in a mess' and 'getting out of the mess', aren't we being very simple-minded in our thinking?
- o If we are being so simple-minded, maybe that's why the world is in such a mess!

o But creating technology surely can't be done by simple-minded people? Therefore only cleverer people make technology. Therefore only cleverer people than us can get us out of the mess we're in.

o Maybe . . .

*Tip*: Using a familiar, safe context can help younger children to feel comfortable with such reasoning games. Try 'The big bad wolf wanted to smash down the three little pigs' houses because . . . ?' and then help the children to use the vocabulary of reasoning.

*Note 1*: Practitioners of formal logic will recognise that all sorts of logical rules are being shaken, rattled and rolled in these games. My justification is that if we want children to become more pow-erful users of logical reasoning, we have to start somewhere and keep it safe and simple. If as a teacher you are interested in learning more about logical reasoning, three very readable yet challenging books are:

Baggini, J. and Stangroom, J. *Do You Think What You think You Think?*, London: Granta, 2006.
van den Brink-Budgen, R., *Critical Thinking for Students*, Oxford: How To Books, 2004.
Weston, A., *A Rulebook for Arguments*, Indianapolis/Cambridge: Hackett Publishing, 2000.

*Note 2*: Playing variations of the '"Because" game' gives the word extra resonance in the children's minds. When a child misbehaves and you ask 'And you did that because?' the child knows he needs to have a really 'sticky' reason to justify his actions!

## NARRATIVE LINES

Most children state with great authority that a story has a begin-ning, a middle and an end. Generally speaking this is true, though only the simplest narratives are so rigidly linear. More often in stories we find back-story and flashbacks, subplots, descriptive digressions, 'future leaps' where events later on in the story are suggested now ('Bond had been lucky so far, but within a month everything would have changed . . . '), 'nested stories' where a secondary tale is recounted within the main narrative, and others.

The vocabulary we have been using so far – 'maybe', 'if . . . then . . .', 'or', etc. – is useful also when we ask children to think about and plan their stories. Many children rely on a simple 'and then . . .' pattern to construct their narrative. Visually this would look like a straight line of paving slabs: the author jumps from one to the next to the next – and then, alas, 'They woke up and it was only a dream.' We can help children to think more subtly about their stories at the planning stage in a number of ways:

- Draw a line on a sheet of paper. This is the basic narrative line. Speak with the child about what might happen in the story. Don't feel you have to start at the beginning. As the child comes up with ideas, have him write them on file cards or Post-its and position them along the line where those events will occur in the tale. This gives the writer both an overview of the whole story plus more detailed references at key points. Open up the narrative options. Pick a card and say 'This could happen, or maybe . . . ?' When the child comes up with another idea, say 'And that would work because . . . ?' to check the reasoning behind the choice. Build on the technique by introducing 'if . . . then . . .', 'so', 'therefore' and other terms to prompt further thinking.
- Story string. This technique works best working one-to-one with a child. Make a string of beads as in Figure 3.4 on page 78. There are thousands of different kinds available now. Lay the strung beads out in front of the child and say 'Let's pretend this is the story we'll think about. Look, here's the beginning, the middle and then the end. All these other beads are to do with the things that happen in between.' Have the child pick up the string and look more closely at the first bead. You might ask 'What does this remind you of – how could the colour and shape of the bead give us an idea to start the story?' Encourage the child just to talk as the ideas come along. If the child seems to be trying too hard

to come up with anything, then make some suggestions of your own: 'Well look, the bead is green and there's a swirly bit in it and it reminds me of water swirling . . . ' The child might then suggest an exciting opening scene such as 'There are two people being sucked into a whirlpool!' Go with the child's ideas as far as possible, guiding and prompting where necessary. What's important at this stage is that the child is gathering impressions and ideas, which can be refined later.

The value of using the story string is that more kinaesthetic children literally 'get their hands' on the things that happen in the narrative. And in all cases discussing the narrative bead by bead focusses the attention and usually generates lots of possibilities.

**Figure 3.4:** Story string

*Tip*: If you want to learn ways of developing narrative lines you might look at:

Bowkett, S. *ALPS StoryMaker: Using Fiction as a Resource for Accelerated Learning*, London: Network Educational Press, 2001.
Bowkett, S. *StoryMaker Catch Pack: Using Genre Fiction as a Resource for Accelerated Learning*, London: Network Educational Press, 2003.

## 3D DIAMOND RANKING

Imagine you have ten different kinds of fruit on the table in front of you – or ten different kinds of chocolates if you want to be really indulgent. The task is to put them in the order in which you would want to eat them. A simple first to tenth ranking might be inadequate. Maybe you'd like to eat the lovely ripe blackberry first, but the cherry and the blueberry come equal second, while the banana, orange and plum really all come third . . .

In the 'diamond ranking' technique you position the fruit to reflect your thinking:

blackberry

cherry, blueberry

banana, orange, plum

apricot, pomegranate

raspberry

kiwi fruit

The shape suggested by such positioning gives the technique its name. Diamond ranking is a more flexible way of organising information than a straightforward linear sequence. It also allows for richer discussion about the positioning of items relative to each other.

- Introduce the diamond ranking technique to children with a familiar example such as the one above. Prepare sets of cards featuring different kinds of fruit and arrange one set according to your preference (using Blu-Tack to stick the cards to a whiteboard – or if you use an electronic board, you might import clip art into text boxes in a Word document. These can then be positioned quite easily on the screen). Explain the reasons for your ranking and then ask the children to use the technique to reflect their choices.
- Use sets of 'top trump' and trading cards as a resource. Many children love to collect such cards. Sets of super hero cards usually come with scores for intelligence, strength, speed, etc. This makes them ideal for positioning using the diamond ranking technique. Cards like these can also be used as the basis for more philosophical discussions of what makes a hero, what is intelligence (and how might we measure it), can someone like Superman truly be brave if he cannot be hurt?
- Increase the challenge of the game by assembling a list of household gadgets that the children have to rank according to 'usefulness' or 'impact on society', or whatever theme you want to emphasise.
- You can diamond rank virtually anything. Ask children to put a list of proverbs in order of wisdom, for instance, or books they've read in order of 'enjoyability'. Always encourage discussion of the reasoning behind the decisions.
- Make the technique more kinaesthetic by using a flight of steps on which ranked items are placed (paying due attention to Health and Safety policy of course). One teacher I know uses Lego bricks and gets the children to construct ziggurats (stepped pyramids), where each layer is a different colour representing different items or ideas.

## IDEAS MATRIX

Create a simple graph template with a vertical and horizontal axis. Ask children to rate, for example, different inventions for recency and usefulness. In this case perhaps the vertical axis could be a timeline and the horizontal axis would mark out 'degrees of usefulness'. Be sure to encourage the children to discuss the concept of 'usefulness' before the activity begins. Some other suggested uses for the matrix are:

- Rate foods for popularity and nutritional value.
- Rate stories for excitement and originality.
- Rate newspapers for depth of coverage and bias.
- Rate poems for emotional impact and difficulty of language.
- Rate household gadgets for complexity and usefulness.
- Rate animals for size and rarity.

## EMOTIONS GRAPH

For this you will need lots of counters of many different colours. Alternatively have the children colour in small squares of paper. Explain that the varied colours stand for different feelings/emotions.

Before going further you might want to explore the links that exist between feelings and colours (see 'What colour is this music?' on page 40). The question 'What colour is anger?' is not a meaningless one even to most younger children: the language is rich with such colour-emotion references. After this discussion some obvious associations will have been made: green for envy, yellow for cowardice, white for fury, blue for misery (as in 'feeling blue'). When unfamiliar connections are made – magnolia for boredom let's say – invite the children to explain why the links might be relevant.

When you have a range of colours and feelings matched, you can use them in these ways:

- Diamond rank feelings from negative to positive and/or frequently felt to rarely felt. Have children literally move the counters around on a sheet of paper.
- Trace the changing feelings of a character in a story. Place counters along a narrative line (a simple beginning–middle–end line) and annotate the events that caused those feelings.

*Tip*: If you want the children to work with their own feelings, be aware that 'issues' can sometimes emerge. Make it clear that if a child wants to use, say, a blue counter for misery, he doesn't have to tell anyone about the cause of that feeling. This is called 'content-free' working, when causes and other details are kept private as the resultant feelings themselves are explored.

- Invite children to plot a 'future graph' for themselves where they deliberately place many positive-coloured counters. This is not about wishful thinking or giving false hope. Arranging the counters/feelings in an imagined future in this way amounts to a powerful statement of intent that primes the subconscious mind to react in that direction (for more practical techniques that combine thinking, creativity and developing emotional resourcefulness, see Bowkett, S. *Self-Intelligence*, London: Network Educational Press, 1999).
- Turning colours up and down. Ask children to imagine red for anger. Now encourage them to 'turn down' the redness in their mind. Tell them to make it pink, then almost white – then get them to begin turning it into a colour that you've decided is very positive (many children link orange with cheerfulness, for instance). Tell the children to hold up (in this case) an orange counter when they've done that mental work. When all the children are holding up their orange counters, do something to distract their attention: blow a whistle or say 'Who's that at the door?' This technique, called a 'break state', instructs the mind that a positive learning process has been completed.

*Note 1*: Thoughts, feelings and physical reactions are linked. Working with thoughts in this way gives children greater control over otherwise automatic emotional reactions. Reinforce positive colour links whenever appropriate. If a child is angry when he comes into the room, give him an orange counter. Then ask the child to change the red in his mind to cheerful orange. When he says he's done that, do a break state then ask how he's feeling now. Often the anger will have lessened or even disappeared.

*Note 2*: Children who are more comfortable with auditory thinking can still do this activity easily. Ask them to match red with a sound and, as that colour changes, get them to change the sound. What would orange cheerfulness sound like? In the case of children who prefer kinaesthetic thinking, have them imagine the red anger as an object they can hold. As the anger changes, get them to change the size, shape, texture and weight of the object in their minds.

- Combine colour–feeling counters with Venn diagrams. Red for anger and (let's say) shiny silver for excitement would be placed in different circles, but the overlap would be the physical indicators of those emotions: quickened pulse, tightening of the muscles perhaps, faster breathing.
- Play the 'Situations game'. Use a picture that depicts an interesting situation involving a number of people – a busy market scene, for instance. Put the picture on the board and have children come up and Blu-Tack colour–feeling counters near different people who, the children think, are expressing those feelings. Invite each contributor to explain his choice of colour–person matching.
- Exploit the colour–feeling links that have been made when you mark children's work. If something that a child writes makes you smile, put a dab of cheerful orange marker pen in the margin next to that sentence. If a link has been established between a colour and the feeling of frustration at not being able to do something, ask children to dab that colour in their workbooks if they feel they have struggled and failed to get something correct or haven't, for whatever reason, been able to do their best. This technique acts as a useful shorthand to emphasise the emotional underpinning of all learning. For, as Plato said, 'Reason must have an adequate emotional base for education to perform its function.' When a child has mastered whatever it was that thwarted him, have him go back in his book and put a cheerful orange sticker over the now-obsolete mark of frustration.

*Note*: Activities like these not only develop children's metacognitive abilities (their ability to notice their own thought processes), but also boost the so-called 'emotional intelligences', one's ability to make links between thoughts, feelings and reactions in oneself and others, and to modify them in a positive direction. For further information see, for example, Goleman, D. *Emotional Intelligence*, London: Bloomsbury, 1996.

## THE NOW SPIDER

Put a picture of an interesting situation on the board – for example, a man running away from a group of other people. Draw four radiating lines coming away from the left of the picture and another four coming away from the right, thus making a vaguely spider-like shape.

Explain that the left of the picture represents the past and the right represents the future. The eight 'legs' of the spider represent things that might have happened (that bring us to the present moment shown in the picture) and what might happen next, leading on from what's occurring now.

Ask the children to come up with four explanations about what might have led to what they see going on in the picture. Annotate the 'past legs'. Then ask for four possible consequences leading on from the action in the picture and, based upon the children's ideas, about what could already have transpired.

*Note*: You may well get more than four plus four ideas, in which case you'll need to increase the number of legs on the spider!

The value of this activity is that it encourages children to perceive their own and others' experiences as snapshots which are part of an ongoing process. It also raises awareness of causes, effects and consequences and, most valuably, creates a way of mapping out options. As the wise old saying has it, 'We are defined by our choices.' The 'NOW spider' gives children a way of reflecting on how they might move on from their present state.

## 3D FLOWCHART

A flowchart is a way of organising information visually to include not just content but also processes for using those ideas. The chart shows the flow of decisions from various options towards a considered conclusion.

Flowcharts make use of standardised symbols and protocols in their construction and use, but these can be kept to a minimum

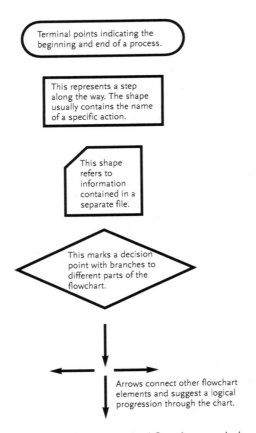

**Figure 3.5:** Some standard flowchart symbols

when introducing the technique and/or using it with younger children. When children are familiar with flowcharts they will have learned an effective planning strategy that can be used in many contexts.

Some of the standard symbols used in flowcharts are shown in Figure 3.5 and a sample flowchart (for planning a story) is shown in Figure 3.6.

*Tip*: Flowcharts can be created easily on a computer. The AutoShapes tool in Microsoft Word on a PC offers a range of 'off-the-peg' flowchart symbols. Print a selection of these on card and laminate them for children to write on using wipe-off marker pens. This gives flowchart-making a 3D element.

## MATCHBOX MYSTERIES

When I was a young boy my friends and I would compete to see who could fit as many small items as possible into a matchbox. This required some ingenuity and lots of diligent searching for suitable bits and pieces. The winner was the one whose matchbox contained the greatest number of items. The only rules of the game were that items could not be duplicated and that each item had to be complete in itself and not a part or fragment. This rule led to some interesting discussions (well, arguments actually) about whether, for example, an apple pip or a watch cog were things in themselves or just parts of a greater whole. It hardly needs me to suggest that such discussions, properly guided, have a fair degree of educational value.

The 'matchbox game' can be adapted in a number of ways to develop children's creativity and thinking skills. You don't have to use matchboxes. Any small containers will do, providing of course that they are all of equal size.

- Fill a chosen container with small items that belong to a hypo-thetical character. Have the children make deductions and inferences about the character as they unpack the box.

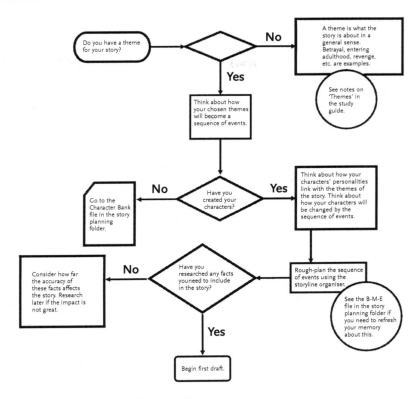

**Figure 3.6:** Section of a flowchart for story planning

*Tip*: Ask groups of children to create their own matchbox characters, then swap for discussion. Keep the boxes of items as a resource to use with other groups in the future.

- A variation of the game is to ask children to list what objects certain fictional characters might put into a matchbox to create a 'mini profile' of themselves.
- Matchbox time capsules. What tiny things would you put into a matchbox to represent our current times? (*Note*: If you think that such a small container limits thinking, allow children to use shoeboxes or something even bigger.) Extend the game

by asking children to list what items you might find in a time capsule that represented, say, late Victorian times or Roman times.

- Matchbox stories. Create a sequence of text boxes on the computer and in each text box write a fragment of a story. Print these, cut them up and put them in the matchbox. Subsequently children have to recreate the narrative sequence. A variation of this game includes snippets of text plus small items in the matchbox. Children are asked to make up a story using as many of the pieces as possible.

# CHAPTER 4

# Jumpstart creative problem solving

The science fiction writer Arthur C. Clarke was once asked why he wrote so much about the future. His reply – 'Because I'm going to spend the rest of my life there.' How much more this applies to the children we teach, who will inherit not only the problems that previous generations have left behind, but must also address new challenges that the future will doubtless bring. With this in mind, giving children strategies for tackling problems of all kinds must surely be one of the fundamental aims of any educational system worthy of the name.

A basic point to be made in this connection is that not all problems can be solved logically and methodically. There is no golden step-by-step approach that will work in all cases. However, the basic elements of creative thinking offer a robust platform both for logical reasoning and for 'Eureka' type off-the-wall solutions. To reiterate, creative thinking depends upon:

- Linking ideas so that knowledge becomes information ('information', formed into greater understandings).
- Taking multiple perspectives; being prepared to examine and explore things from many different viewpoints.

Central to this ethos is the notion of play (which children usually know how to do very well). Interestingly, the roots of the word come from the Old English *plegan*, to exercise oneself, and correspond to the old Dutch term *pleyen*, dance). Creative problem solving exercises the mind in a dance of possibilities.

While the stand-alone activities in this book mean that it can be 'dipped into' at any point, you will appreciate that all of the chapters of the book are interlinked and complementary. However, here are a few more games and techniques that focus specifically on problem solving.

## WAYS OF DOING – STRATEGIC THINKING

There is often not a single solution to a problem but a number of possible solutions. Each one may be reached by approaching the difficulty in a different way. Each 'way of doing' is a strategy: strategic thinking in this general sense considers strategies in the plural. It is true that sometimes there is a 'best' way of overcoming a problem and that sometimes there is only one way. Learning challenges of this kind need to be balanced with problems requiring an active search for alternative solutions.

- Highlight situations where a particular way of doing is obviously the most effective one and examine why this strategy works best. Begin with something simple like a recipe. Why are the steps arranged in that particular order? What might be the effect of putting some of the steps in a different order?
- Show the children maps and ask them to plan a route between two points. Encourage them to consider various routes and to settle on the one that they think works best, for reasons they can explain.
- Invite the children to discuss ways of solving the following problem: 'Using a barometer, how do you measure the height of a tall block of flats?'

*Note*: This problem forms the basis of a famous anecdote where a physics student was asked this question in an examination at the University of Copenhagen. He suggested that a string be tied to the barometer, which was then lowered to the ground. Measuring the length of the string used plus the length of the barometer would give the answer.

The examiners didn't accept this answer as one showing much understanding of physics, so they invited the student to an interview to suggest a more satisfactory reply. Upon prompting, the student said:

> Firstly, you could take the barometer up to the roof of the skyscraper, drop it over the edge, and measure the time it takes to reach the ground. The height of the building can then be worked out from the formula H = 0.5g × t squared. But bad luck on the barometer.
>
> Or if the sun is shining you could measure the height of the barometer, then set it on end and measure the length of its shadow. Then you measure the length of the skyscraper's shadow, and thereafter it is a simple matter of proportional arithmetic to work out the height of the skyscraper.
>
> But if you wanted to be highly scientific about it, you could tie a short piece of string to the barometer and swing it like a pendulum, first at ground level and then on the roof of the skyscraper. The height is worked out by the difference in the gravitational restoring force T = 2 pi sqr root (l/g).
>
> Or if the skyscraper has an outside emergency staircase, it would be easier to walk up it and mark off the height of the skyscraper in barometer lengths, then add them up.
>
> If you merely wanted to be boring and orthodox about it, of course, you could use the barometer to measure the air pressure on the roof of the skyscraper and on the ground, and convert the difference in millibars into feet to give the height of the building.
>
> But since we are constantly being encouraged to exercise independence of mind and apply scientific methods, undoubtedly the best way would be to knock on the janitor's door and say to him 'I will give you this nice new barometer if you tell me the height of this block of flats.'

The student was Niels Bohr, who went on to win a Nobel Prize for Physics in 1922. (*Source*: www.snopes.com/college/exam/barometer.asp)

## THE LUCKILY/UNLUCKILY GAME

This game develops quick thinking and gives children the opportunity to look at ideas, issues, problems, etc. from at least two viewpoints. It can also be used to create story plots.

- Introduce the game with a simple idea, such as 'On his way home from school Saeed slipped over in the park. Luckily he fell on grass, so didn't hurt himself. But unluckily he got grass stains on his shirt . . . '
- Then ask the children to join in. You may want to pick the first raised hand, or choose ideas table by table or child by child. Say 'Unluckily Saeed got grass stains on his shirt. Luckily, though . . . ?' A child might say 'It wasn't his best shirt!' You say 'Luckily it wasn't his best shirt – but unluckily . . . ?'
- The game continues either until the 'story' reaches some kind of natural conclusion or the class run out of ideas or, more likely, you put a time limit on it.
- Add a kinaesthetic element by playing the game in the hall or some other open space. Mark a line on the floor. One side is the 'luckily' side, the other the 'unluckily' side. Split the class into two and have one group stand on each side of the line. Begin the game – 'On Saturday Jessica lost all of her pocket money. But luckily . . . ?' Only children from the 'unluckily' side of the line can contribute ideas. When a child answers, he can hop over to the other side of the line. Children starting from the 'unluckily' side must contribute 'luckily' ideas and hop to that side when they have done so. The game finishes when every child ends up on the opposite side of the line.
- The downside of this variation of the game is that the children who contributed ideas first must then stay silent to keep their place on the side where they want to end up. You can overcome this problem by suggesting that any child can contribute as many ideas as they like, moving across the line several times, but they must end up on the right side of the line – the side opposite the one they started from.

*Tip*: You can also put a time limit on the game so that children can't move endlessly from one side to the other. Another option is to give each child three counters as tokens. Each time a child's idea is picked (so he moves across the line) he must give up a token. Supplying children with an odd number of tokens means that each child ends up on the correct side of the line when the last token is spent.

- Another variation is to have all the children starting from one end of the hall or open space. Arrange the children into a number of teams. Begin the game. Pick the first hand that goes up each time. When a child's idea is selected she takes one big step forward. The first team to have all its members reach the far end of the hall by contributing ideas wins.
- Use the game to rehearse children's understanding of story genre. If you are looking at fantasy stories, for example, tell the children beforehand that they must use ideas from the fantasy tales (or myths and legends) that you've looked at. So, 'Once long ago Pegasus the winged horse lost the power of flight. Luckily . . . ?' 'Hercules said he would help Pegasus to find out why!' 'But unluckily . . . ?' 'Unluckily Zeus the Father of the gods forbade this . . . '
- Make the game more challenging by preparing flashcards beforehand showing pictures or key words related to the topic that you want to rehearse. Children must incorporate what's on the flashcard into their answer.

*Tip*: The flashcards can also show connectives, which children must build into their replies. So 'Unluckily Hercules couldn't help Pegasus because Zeus forbade it [show flashcard, e.g. 'meanwhile'].' 'But luckily, meanwhile, Hera told Hercules to go ahead and she would deal with Zeus.'

- Use the 'Luckily/unluckily game' to explore topical issues. Insist that children must give reasonable answers that show some understanding of the issue. So:

  o Luckily my dustbin is emptied every week, so the rubbish doesn't overflow.
  o But unluckily it's all taken to a landfill site to be buried.
  o Luckily, however, some of that rubbish can be recycled.
  o Unluckily, though, not all of it can be recycled.

- o But luckily there is still plenty of space in landfill sites.
- o Unluckily that space will one day run out.
- o But luckily we are finding new ways of dealing with rubbish. (Here you might pause the game to ask the class about what these new ways are.)

## 'WHAT IF . . . ?' CIRCLE

Draw a circle on the board and give the children a 'What if . . . ?' situation to talk about, such as 'What if oil was going to run out in five years' time?' Ask them to reflect on how this problem would affect them personally – in other words, you are looking for personal/local/small-scale responses.

Put some or all of these responses on the board inside the circle, using the elements of mind mapping if you wish. These are:

- Different categories of information arranged in different parts of the visual field.
- Colour coding for easy visual reference.
- The use of key words around which further information is gathered.
- Making logical/creative links between previously separate ideas.

Now draw a larger circle around the first one and ask the children to discuss the problem as it might affect their whole neighbourhood. Map the responses. Put another circle around the other two – how might the issue affect the entire country? Finally in the largest, outer circle – how might the issue affect the whole world?

The point of this technique is that it offers children a way of organising ideas visually and in terms of scale, while suggesting a link between the global and the personal. The children can literally see how their responses 'ripple out' into the world at large, and how things that happen on the world stage have direct relevance to their own lives.

## LETTERS TO THE EDITOR

Prepare for this activity by building a resource from the letters pages of popular newspapers. Ideally collect letters from various papers on the same theme(s). The focus of the activity is not so much to find out where the children stand on the issues (although you can do that as well, of course), but to look more closely at the semantics (meanings) of the language. Help the children to look for things like:

- Generalised statements which beg many questions/generalisations based upon one or a couple of possibly isolated events.
- 'Deletion' of information, or statements that (perhaps deliberately) express a partial truth.
- The use of opinion, which may be masquerading as fact. Look for evidence supporting such statements.
- The use of exaggeration.
- The use of emotive language.
- Negative filtering, where positive aspects of a situation are deliberately left out (this being a kind of deletion).
- All-or-nothing viewpoints or either/or situations.
- The use of statistics out of context and/or invalidly to bolster the writer's opinion.

Note that all of these may be incorporated into the writer's point of view and technically constitute bias. In terms of a thinking skills agenda, analysing for bias is one of the so-called 'critical thinking skills'. Practising this is an important way of developing children's logical reasoning abilities. (See Fogarty, R. and Bellanca, J. *Teach Them Thinking*, Arlington Heights, IL: Skylight Professional Development, 1986.)

## VIEWPOINTS

Mark three spots on the floor, of different colours or labelled A, B and C. Select an issue for discussion. Advise the children that whoever stands on spot A must argue for the proposition, whoever stands on spot B must argue against it, while whoever stands on spot C is a 'neutral observer' who must hold back his own opinions and beliefs and consider the arguments of A and B on their merits.

Give the A and B children time to prepare their ideas, perhaps with the support of classmates who can add to the stock of ideas and help to firm up the arguments. Have the children stand on their spots. Each presents his case while the other listens. Then allow a certain time for more open discussion between the two participants. Meanwhile C is listening carefully and judging which ideas/arguments are well supported by reasons and facts, which opinions and beliefs are not, etc.

As a plenary you can invite the rest of the class to join in the discussion. Ideas can be recorded on scraps of paper and subsequently used with the cut ups technique (see page 65).

Vary the activity by inviting children to stand on a spot and argue from a viewpoint opposite to the one they actually believe in. Point out that effective discussion often involves seeing things from another's viewpoint so that counter-arguments can be considered beforehand.

Vary the activity further by asking each of the three children – A, B and C – to change positions each time you blow a whistle, for instance. Each child therefore has the experience of all of the viewpoints; for, against and neutral.

*Tip*: Most if not all of us have opinions about all kinds of issues. The kinds of techniques I have been describing raise children's awareness of their own and others' opinions and invite reflection on why those opinions are held. Opinions that can be justified by reasoned argument and supported by facts are always more powerful.

In contrast to the above, initiate a 'No Judgement Day' with your class. On this day, refrain from having any opinions at all or making any value judgements about people or the ideas you encounter. This is more difficult to do than you might imagine, but how wonderfully refreshing it is to be freed from the burden of judgement.

## DECISION ALLEY

This is a well-known technique for exploring issues and areas of argument. Discuss a chosen issue beforehand (using techniques described above if you wish). Now divide the class into two groups, each group supporting an opposite viewpoint. Each child will become responsible for an idea that supports his group's stand-point. It may be an opinion, fact or belief.

Tell the children that soon they will be asked to present their argu-ment to another group. Ask them to decide in which order they will present the ideas supporting their standpoint. When this has been done, use a large open space and have the children stand in two lines facing one another. The children in each line are to stand in the order they have previously agreed.

Invite the children from the 'guest group' to walk slowly between the two lines. As they do, your children must whisper their ideas to the passing guests. Once the guest group have walked through decision alley, ask them if what they have heard:

- Strengthened their personal viewpoint.
- Weakened their personal viewpoint.
- Caused them to change their mind.
- Had no effect.

As a plenary, have all of the children involved in the game discuss the whole issue as they analyse the veracity and persuasive power of the ideas they have experienced.

## FINDING THE BALANCE

This is a game that develops the skill of *mediation*. The word derives from the Latin, meaning 'to be in the middle'.

To introduce the game, ask for two volunteers. The rest of the class will observe. Mark a line on the floor. Have the volunteers stand one at each end of the line. Decide what issue is to be discussed – 'Four-by-fours are dangerous, highly polluting and should be banned!' Ask one volunteer to argue in agreement of this idea and the other to be vehemently opposed, i.e. someone who loves and cherishes his four-by-four.

You may want at this stage to point out that people have the right to own large vehicles but that yes, traffic is polluting and can be dangerous. Introduce the notion of *compromise*. This is a 'settlement of differences' and comes from the Latin, meaning 'to promise mutually'.

Ask a child at one end of the line to suggest something he could do to help settle the differences between himself and the other volunteer. Use the other children in the class to discuss the merits of this proposal if you wish. Find out how the other volunteer feels about the 'offer'. If she is not willing to accept the proposal, ask her to justify why. The justification has to be reasonable to the child at the other end of the line and, ideally, to most or all of the observers.

If the proposal is accepted, ask the volunteer who suggested it to take a measured step forward along the line. If the proposal is not accepted for good reasons, the child does not move.

Now it's the turn of the volunteer at the opposite end of the line to offer a step towards compromise. The same procedure applies.

As the game progresses the whole issue is explored, together with a number of reasonable steps that can be taken to achieve a workable compromise. The activity concludes when the two volunteers are close enough together to shake hands on a settlement.

## 'SMILEMMAS'

Literally speaking a *di*lemma is a no-win or lose-lose situation. It is thought the word comes from the Greek, meaning 'involving two assumptions'. This is an interesting idea, because an assumption is often a conclusion reached without reference to the outside world and/or something taken for granted. When things are taken for granted they are not analysed, reflected upon or questioned.

Many dilemmas, therefore, can be opened out and even resolved by identifying and questioning the assumptions on which they are built. Sometimes an assumption is found to be illusory or wrong, and the dilemma itself evaporates. A simple example is 'Steve, either you turn your music down or you can't listen to it at all!' The dilemma here is that, whatever happens, Steve or the complainant will lose out. The assumption lies in the either/or viewpoint in which the issue is framed. This does not reflect the reality of the situation and the 'dilemma' could perhaps be resolved by:

- Steve using headphones.
- Steve only playing his music loud when the complainant is not around.
- Soundproofing his room.
- Reaching a compromise by Steve turning his music down a little.
- The complainant using earplugs.

In the field of reasoning there is something known as a *false dilemma*, where the claim is made that either A or B is true (when in fact both could be false or where C, D, E, etc. also exist as part of the issue). The false reasoning that occurs in this situation is:

- Either claim A or B is true.
- Claim A is false.
- Therefore claim B is true.

This is like saying that either one plus one equals three or one plus one equals five. Because one plus one does not equal three then one plus one equals five must be right. Note though that when there are only two absolutes in an issue and one of them is demonstrated to be false then the other is true . . . Steve is either dead or alive. Steve is not dead, therefore he is alive.

There is no shortage of dilemmas to choose from (a) to test their assumptions and (b) to work towards turning them into smilemmas, where everyone involved gets at least some benefit.

This resolution can come about through more thoroughly exploring the problem, seeing the situation from other people's viewpoints, mediation and compromise.

Here are a few dilemmas that you might ask the children to turn into win-win smilemmas:

- There is a water shortage and the water company asks all customers not to water their gardens, take baths or otherwise use water unnecessarily. Your friend puts forward what he feels is the very reasonable argument that if he cuts his water usage by 50 per cent he isn't going to get a 50 per cent reduction in his water bill, is he? Apart from that, he suggests that if he waters his garden that consumption is only a tiny amount that will not really add to the crisis. Besides, if he doesn't water his garden a little today, tomorrow he'll have to water it more to prevent his plants from dying.
- Offering state-funded benefits to people who are out of work is a social dilemma. The fact is that often the benefits an unemployed person gets (particularly if (s)he has a family) amount to more than the wage that could be earned. What incentive is there, then, to go out and get a job?
- Fish supplies are dwindling at an alarming rate. Some fishermen have been told to reduce their catches by half. However, catching this smaller quantity of fish means that the fishermen will not make a living wage and so go out of business. In any case, most fishermen ignore the quota rule anyway, so why should I as a fisherman obey it? The extra fish I catch is hardly going to make the problem much worse.
- The school is spending more money than it's receiving in funding. The only option is to sell off the playing fields to property developers.

## ICEBERG THINKING

Here's a puzzle. Imagine a room locked from the inside. All of the windows are also locked. A stout wooden beam runs the length of the room. Hanging from the beam is a rope, tied into a noose at the end, from which hangs a dead man. There is a large puddle on the carpet beneath him.

If you know the answer to this mystery, pretend you don't for a few moments. What questions could you ask in an endeavour to find a solution? My immediate questions would be:

- Is the man the only person in the room?
- What is the liquid underneath him?
- Was his hanging deliberate?

Other questions of course can arise from the answers to these. 'Iceberg thinking' raises our awareness that what we are told is usually only part of the picture, or the tip of the iceberg. Based on what we are told we make assumptions, inferences and deductions that lead us to jump to conclusions or reach a solution in a more reasonable way.

A useful template to offer the children is to draw a triangle (a stylised iceberg) and mark off the peak. That portion contains what we know. Now mark off about a third of what remains. That portion represents what we think we know (assume, infer, etc.). The rest of the iceberg is reserved for 'What we need to ask'.

When you use this template with the class, use the children's assumptions, inferences and speculations as the basis for further questions that will help to clarify the situation. Emphasise that even if those questions cannot be answered, asking them in the first place is a valuable learning process.

*Note*: And in case you were wondering, the solution to the opening puzzle is that the man wanted to punish himself for some wrongdoing. He arranged for a large block of ice to be brought to the room, stood on this to put the noose around his neck and secure the rope's other end to the beam, then waited for the ice to melt in order to suffer a slow death by strangulation.

# THE DILEMMAS GAME

This game is a fun way of combining and consolidating a number of the above activities.

- Have the children draw a winding path on a large sheet of paper or card. Divide the path into, say, 50 segments and number the segments.
- Help the children devise a narrative that will act as the context for the dilemmas and problems they will face. One popular example I have used is a journey to a 'lost world' along the lines of Arthur Conan Doyle's famous novel of the same name, but of course there are many alternatives.
- Once the basic storyline is agreed, create a number of characters – five or six to start with. Use the PIN technique for fleshing out each character: think of a few *positive* characteristics, a few *negative* qualities and a few *interesting* attributes.
- Create a list of the equipment that the adventurers will take with them on their expedition. Deciding on this list can be a useful exercise in logical reasoning and problem solving in itself.
- At this point you can either think of some dilemmas yourself, or have the children do it. The dilemmas will amount to problems and crises that the explorers are to face, and which will be resolved by the kinds of techniques we have looked at in this book. Examples of such dilemmas might be:

  - As you move upriver towards Prehistoric Plateau you hear people shouting from either side of the riverbank. You see two children on one side and their parents on the other. Both groups are in danger – the children from hungry crocodiles that have cut off their retreat; the parents from savage tribal warriors who are approaching with spears and blowpipes. You know you only have time to reach one side or the other of the river. Who do you choose to save?
  - During your exploration of the cave network in the cliffs of Prehistoric Plateau you come across a chasm plunging down to great depths. The chasm is spanned by a rickety wooden bridge. While the rest of the party sleep for the night, you and another character cross the bridge and soon discover a cache of hidden jewels.

*Dilemma A*: Do you tell the rest of the party about this treasure, knowing you will have to split it among them?

*Dilemma B*: Holding the torch you re-cross the bridge to safety, followed by your companion who is carrying the bag of jewels. When (s)he is half way across, the far side of the rickety bridge comes loose. Your companion manages to hold on with one hand, desperately clutching the bag of jewels with the other. You know there is time only for your companion to throw the jewels to you or for him/her to let go of the bag and cling with both hands, allowing you to arrange a rescue. What advice do you give?

*Dilemma C*: If you choose to take the jewels – as you grab the bag your companion tells you that his/her partner is dying from an illness that can be cured by an expensive drug. The jewels will pay for that medicine. Does this alter your decision?

o The group's explorations on Prehistoric Plateau reveal a wonderland of creatures thought to be long extinct – dinosaurs, pterosaurs, ancient plants. It is obviously a thriving but still very fragile environment. You all realise that when you take specimens back to civilisation your fame and fortune will be secured. But you also know that revealing the existence of the plateau will bring more explorers, fortune-seekers and developers here. This will most likely result in the destruction of the creatures you have discovered. What do you decide to do? Supposing that you wanted to keep the plateau's existence a secret, but some of your companions did not, what arguments would you use to try and persuade them otherwise?

# CHAPTER 5
# Jumpstart creative wordplay

Children's ability to manipulate language is a measure of their 'linguistic intelligence' (to use a term coined by the psychologist Howard Gardner.) Gardner's well-known 'multiple intelligences' model of the mind provides powerful insights that can guide our classroom practice. Gardner asserts that we are born with a number of potentials or talents and that these are innate in us and hard-wired in the brain. Children's ability to become more linguistically intelligent depends upon the richness of their language environment (at home and at school), and their preparedness to explore words and the effects of language in a playful way, driven by curiosity and a sense of adventure and fun.

Children 'own' language no less than Shakespeare did. Furthermore language is not set in stone. It is a flexible, fluid, ever-evolving thing. Words appear, change and vanish as the world itself changes. The usefulness of language is a function of its effectiveness in communicating within a range of contexts. 'Text language' for instance – often a controversial topic with those who want to see grammatical standards maintained – is a practical and useful style within its context of use. It is not right or wrong or good or bad, but more or less practical for its chosen purposes.

What I am trying to suggest here is that a creative approach to language – wordplay – will develop our children's ability to use words powerfully. This must be rooted in the realisation that linguistic structures and styles are like a box of instruments, and that the linguistically intelligent child knowingly chooses a particular instrument to do a particular job.

*Sources*:

Bryson, B. *Mother Tongue*, London: Penguin Books, 1990.

Gardner, H. *Multiple Intelligences: The Theory in Practice*, New York: Basic Books, 1993.

## 'THIS PRODUCT COMES WITH A LIFETIME GUARANTEE' – LOOKING AT LANGUAGE

Does language ever reflect reality, or only represent the surface structure of endless realities? The words we read and hear and say and write are necessarily only part of the bigger picture. Perhaps in every case meanings are manipulated, either unwittingly or deliberately, to create certain impressions. I suggest that one very useful approach to the study of language bears this in mind. Take a look at these examples:

1.  This product comes with a lifetime guarantee.
2.  Worried about thinning hair? I was, but not any more. Try new improved HairGrow today.
3.  There are three errors in this sentance
4.  You can't trust city people.
5.  I never make generalisations.

Before I comment on these, note down your own observations or the questions that come to mind about these statements.

1.  What does the 'lifetime guarantee' refer to? The lifetime of the product, the lifetime of the company or your lifetime? What are the terms of the guarantee? The product might come with a guarantee, but does the guarantee refer to that product (or is this being just too cynical?).
2.  The 'I' in the second sentence doesn't mention that (s)he was worried about his or her own hair, or indeed whether the hair was thinning at all. The reference to the HairGrow remedy need have no connection with the second statement.

3. The first error is the misspelling of 'sentence'. The second error is the missing full stop at the end. The third error is to claim that the sentence contains three errors when in fact it contains only those two . . . Except that in itself is an error, which means that the sentence does contain three . . . Except that in pointing that out it means the sentence only contains *two* errors . . . So here we have a paradox that takes us round in an endless loop.

4. This statement is an opinion based on a generalisation. The 'you' might mean 'one' or could perhaps refer to you personally. The way to deal with such generalisations is to ask for specific information. How exactly do you define 'city people'? On which particular cities and people are you basing your view? In what sense can't 'city people' be trusted?

5. This statement is a generalisation in itself and therefore a paradox. In saying I never make generalisations, I have made a generalisation.

*Tip*: An internet search for paradox or generalisation will bring up further examples. Look also at the letters pages in newspapers for more material to examine. Find a sentence a day for your children to examine, analyse, ponder about and otherwise play with.

## ADJECTIVAL NAMES

This activity links adjectives with nouns in various ways.

- Using examples like Honest John, Diamond Mick and Light-footed Louisa as examples, make two lists, one of first names and the other of adjectives and adjectival phrases. Have the children cross-match adjectives with nouns, select the ones that work best and make up stories as to how those characters acquired their names. You can also ask the children to attach suitable adjectives to their own first names in a way that reflects some positive quality – Sunny Steve, Enthusiastic Emma, Resourceful Ramesh, etc.

*Tip*: This is a good opportunity to look into the origins of names. Many family names derive from occupations (Smith, Baker,

Cooper, etc.), traits and qualities (e.g. Roberts from the Old German words meaning 'fame' and 'bright') and places (Green from the Old English word for a village green). The study can usefully be extended to look at the origins of names from other cultures.

- To create character names for fantasy stories, make a list of some suitable nouns – moon, sword, fire, sky, wind, stone, etc. and another list of nouns that have a 'verbal force' such as flyer, slayer, hewer, leaper, dancer, wanderer, etc. Then mix and match . . . Moonleaper, Stonehewer, Skydancer.

*Tip*: This activity can serve as a useful introduction to the *kenning*. This is an Anglo-Saxon literary device, familiar in poetry, where a new noun or noun phrase is created to replace a more familiar one. Some examples are: sword = battlefriend or, more grimly, widow-maker; the sky = the swan's road; plague = deathbringer. Note the metaphorical nature of many kennings and the way in which they force one to look at things in new ways. Making up kennings gives children the opportunity to think more deeply and creatively about the people, places and objects they see every day.

- An engaging technique is the group or class kenning. Here an object or creature, is selected and each child or working group creates a kenning to describe it. These are collected and rearranged so that the kenning-poem flows well. Here's an example created by a Y5 mixed-ability class:

> Tree tapper, grub grabber, writhing-maggot muncher –
> Bright blood-red woodland dweller.
>
> Fresh grass-green-leaf hunter, spotted soarer –
> Flying fantasy flapping furiously.
>
> Feathery-featured, glisten-eyed small speckled songster.

Solution: a woodpecker.

- For more ideas on creating genre-based names, see my *StoryMaker Catch Pack* (see reference on page 79).
- Place names form another useful source for creative wordplay. Look through a dictionary of place names (see, for instance,

Ekwall, E. *The Concise Oxford Dictionary of English Place-names*, fourth edition, Oxford: 1981), select some appropriate examples and ask the children to make up stories explaining how the places acquired their names:

- *Monyash*. This actually means 'many an ash (tree)'. I wonder why the ash trees were so important originally that the place was named after them? Some children read the place name as 'Money Ash' – now there's an opening for any number of fascinating stories!
- *Market Harborough*. Playing about with this gives 'market at the rough harbour'. What was it about the harbour that was so rough? And why? What kind of market might you find there?
- *Bicknor*. 'The slope belonging to Bica'. Who might Bica have been? What important or dramatic or terrible thing happened in Bica's life that it was remembered in the name of this place?

*Tip*: Encourage the children to research the true origins of place names after they've made up their stories.

## A MEDLEY OF WORD GAMES

My first is in fish but not in the sea.

The idea of this game is to work out which letter each line is talking about. When you put the secret letters from all the lines together they spell a word. Here's an example:

My first is in fish but not in the sea.

My second in bird but not in a tree,

My third is in doors but not in a hall.

My last is in everything but not nothing at all.

My whole cannot die as long as it has food? What am I?

Answer: fire.

Here are a few more to puzzle over.

My first is in mage but never in wizard.

My second's in goblin and also in lizard.

My third is in night but not in day.

My last is in field, you won't find it in hay.

Answer: mind.

My first is in planet and also in star.

My second's in near and also afar.

My next is in iron but never in steel.

My last's not in food but always in meal.

Answer: tail.

My first is in river but never in lake.

My second's in cooking but not found in cake.

My third's in surprise and also in shock.

My last is in sheep but not once in flock.

Answer: rose.

Examples can be as easy or difficult as you like. They don't need to rhyme and there need be only one letter difference between the pairs of words. So for example:

My first is in man but never in men.

My second's in can but not in can't.

My third is in on but never in in.

My fourth is in me but you won't find me in be.

Answer: atom.

Creating such puzzles develops attention, concentration and spelling.

## Acrostics

An acrostic has been called 'a poem with a word down the side'. The term comes from the Greek, meaning 'end' plus 'a row or line of verse'. Here's an example using 'wordsmith':

Wonderment in seeing

Ordinary people, places, moments in my life

Rolled around the mind,

Dropped carefully on the page,

Stitched in my memory;

Many beautiful things

Interest me,

Threaded on the

Heart of my life.

Simple ones can be made from the children' names:

Smiling most of the time

Always ready to help

Raring to go!

Adventurous and

Happy as the day is long.

## Call My Bluff

'Call My Bluff' was the name of a popular TV quiz programme. There were two teams. A person from one team would show the other a word (usually a very obscure one!) and offer three definitions, only one of which was correct. If the opposing team picked the correct definition they scored a point.

Ask teams of children to search through a dictionary to find some unfamiliar words and then (the fun bit) think up two false definitions to put with the definition that the dictionary gives you.

For instance, the word is 'ORTHOCLASE'. Does this mean:

a) A special way of looking after your teeth?
b) A kind of mineral?
c) A moving pavement that you find mainly in California?

You can play the game the other way round, by giving the other team a definition and asking them to match the right word to it. For instance:

> Is an animal with no backbone and three pairs of legs (a) an insect (b) an invertebrate (c) an instant?

## Word search

Create a box filled with squares and help the children to build their own word search. Giving the search a theme helps to generate suitable words, such as the theme of 'animals' in our example (see Figure 5.1 on page 112). Decide beforehand whether to allow words written backwards (as in 'wren' in our example), diagonally (as in 'panda' in our example) etc. Write in your chosen words first, then fill the remaining squares with random letters.

You can vary the difficulty of the game by giving the box more or fewer squares/longer or shorter words. You can also create a challenge by putting in a word that's related to the theme. In our example it's a word that is not an animal itself but has something to do with an animal ('web' is the answer).

Other animals to find are: bison, eagle, elephant, emu, giraffe, hedgehog, kangaroo, meerkat, possum and whale.

| N | O | S | I | B | G | M | S | A | L | R | C |
|---|---|---|---|---|---|---|---|---|---|---|---|
| J | F | O | O | Z | P | E | M | U | O | Y | P |
| M | N | N | T | G | X | A | O | E | R | U | O |
| E | K | E | N | I | H | G | N | V | E | E | S |
| E | G | R | D | R | P | L | M | D | K | L | S |
| R | H | W | H | A | L | E | F | E | A | Q | U |
| K | U | I | E | F | F | C | Q | A | N | S | M |
| A | H | T | K | F | L | W | E | B | G | U | A |
| T | J | L | O | E | L | E | P | H | A | N | T |
| P | M | E | N | X | E | D | U | C | R | M | W |
| Q | F | J | V | A | P | I | R | L | O | A | M |
| H | E | D | G | E | H | O | G | Y | O | I | S |

**Figure 5.1:** Word search

## Kennings

A kenning is a descriptive phrase, usually just two words long, that dates back to the time of the Vikings and the Celts. The word kenning itself means 'to name after'. So for instance in 'kenning-speak' the sea could be called the whale's road, while the sun might be named the world-candle.

Help the children to create two-word descriptions of ordinary objects. Here are some to start you off:

**Table 5.1:** Kennings

| Object | Kenning | Another example |
|--------|---------|-----------------|
| Fork | Food-lifter | Meat-piercer |
| Wife | Bargain-hunter | Life-partner |
| Book | Knowledge-giver | |
| Falcon | Sky-warrior | |
| Sun | | |
| iPod | | |
| | Mouse-stalker | |
| | Distance-eater | |

Once children are familiar with the idea they can create longer phrases and put them together into more elaborate descriptions. What for instance, is being described here?

Tree tapper, grub grabber, writhing-maggot muncher,
Bright blood-red woodland dweller.

## Odd one out – and in

Use the lists below and ask your children the following questions:

a) beech–elm–violet–fern–orchid–pine
b) gold–glass–bronze–slate–iron–lead
c) town–city–village–utopia–park–suburb
d) tea–coke–juice–beer–water–coffee
e) carpenter–miner–teacher–electrician–baker–barber
f) ant–bear–cat–deer–eel–fox

- Which is the odd one out in each list, and why?
- Now pick a different item from a list and decide why *that* could be the odd one out.
- Put the animals in list (f) in order of size.

- Put the jobs in list (e) in order of importance. (This can lead to some great discussions!)
- Put the items in any list in alphabetical order.
- Pick a list and say what all of the items have in common.
- Pick an item from any list and find something from any other list that is connected in some way.

*Tip*: This is more of a challenge if you roll a dice to choose your two lists and one item from each of them.

## CONNECTIVE CHAINS

This is an improvisational game where the object is to keep a story rolling, however ridiculous it might become, by the use of connectives.

First prepare a list of connectives that the children can refer to: and, but, namely, such as, for example, in other words, that is, therefore, because, similarly, firstly . . . secondly etc., then, moreover, in addition to, also, likewise, besides, later, most importantly, furthermore, nevertheless, however, still, rather, despite that, yet, after all, conversely, on the other hand, at the same time, consequently, so that, in order that, hence, consequently, in conclusion, so, as a result, finally . . .

Explain to the children that they can invent characters and situations as they go along and use any connective more than once. But however fantastical or wacky the story becomes, the connectives themselves have to make a valid link between statements: it would not be valid to say 'The quick brown fox jumps over a lazy dog, consequently shoes are pink'.

Then start the ball rolling:

> The cat sat on the mat in addition to the mouse called George. At the same time, George's wife Ophelia Mouse was cleaning round them, because they were expecting a visit from Great Uncle Montgomery Mouse later. Furthermore, other members of the family were going to arrive soon as the result of an urgent message that George had emailed the day before . . .

And so on. The unexpected twists and turns of the story are likely to keep children's interest and enthusiasm going as they rehearse a wide variety of connectives.

*Tip*: You can add a kinaesthetic element and make the game more challenging by writing the connectives on pieces of paper, which are put into an envelope or bag. Split the class into two teams. Each child takes one connective out of the bag and must decide when to use it. Set the story rolling. Children from either team 'jump in' with their connective. The team that uses all its connectives first is the winner.

## A MELANGE OF MOTIFS

In a literary sense a motif is an image, sound, action or object that develops the theme of a narrative and can affect the tone or mood of the writing. In the field of textiles a motif is a smaller element in a larger work; a knitted or stitched pattern within the greater fabric. This definition is useful when we consider that textiles and text share the same origin, coming from the Latin *texere*, 'to weave'. Used metaphorically in discussing writing or thinking we can talk about:

- The raw material we need to work on
- Spinning a yarn
- Unpicking a knotty problem
- Being in a tangle
- Woolly thinking
- Losing or picking up the thread of an idea
- Tying up loose ends
- Creating and repeating a pattern
- A patchwork of ideas
- Ironing out the wrinkles
- A web of thoughts/an association web
- A tissue woven of many threads

The immediate value of such metaphors is that they allow us to think of abstract concepts in concrete terms. It's easier for children to 'grasp' (another 'physical' metaphor) the idea of getting into a tangle over a task or problem than having some difficulties.

115

Motifs such as the examples shown in Table 5.2 are also 'artfully vague'. This means that we are given a specific piece of information, but it is sufficiently nebulous to beg a number of questions. If we select 'gift', for instance, we might want to know what the gift is, who gave it and why, whether it is in return for something also given and so on. Artful vagueness is an example of flexibility within a structure, mentioned elsewhere in the book, which is an important principle in stimulating and developing children's creative thinking.

**Table 5.2:** Melange of motifs

| | | | | | | | |
|---|---|---|---|---|---|---|---|
| 1. | Adventurer | 2. | Guide | 3. | Wise One | 4. | Prince(ss) |
| 5. | Ruler | 6. | Witch/Wizard | 7. | Guardian | 8. | Wanderer |
| 9. | Hero(ine) | 10. | Beast | 11. | Enchanter | 12. | Maiden |
| 13. | Lover | 14. | Keeper | 15. | Captor | 16. | Liberator |
| 17. | Learner | 18. | Mentor | 19. | Companion | 20. | Trial |
| 21. | Quest | 22. | Mirror | 23. | Blade | 24. | Barrier |
| 25. | Road | 26. | Gift | 27. | Theft | 28. | Descending |
| 29. | Ascending | 30. | Earth | 31. | Air | 32. | Fire |
| 33. | Water | 34. | Metal | 35. | Wood | 36. | Stone |
| 37. | Higher/Lower | 38. | Coincidence | 39. | Circle | 40. | Repetition |
| 41. | Pattern | 42. | Order/Chaos | 43. | Disguise | 44. | Mountain |
| 45. | Pool | 46. | Shore | 47. | Threshold | 48. | Woods |
| 49. | Darkness/Light | 50. | Morass | 51. | Tower | 52. | Labyrinth |
| 53. | Bridge | 54. | Crossway | 55. | House | 56. | City |
| 57. | Door/Gateway | 58. | Key | 59. | Hut/Hovel | 60. | Palace |
| 61. | Uncharted Way | 62. | High Seas | 63. | Life/Death | 64. | Sleep |
| 65. | Wish | 66. | Bond | 67. | Mother | 68. | Father |
| 69. | Siblings | 70. | Great/Less | 71. | Trickster | 72. | Maker |
| 73. | Giant | 74. | Creature | 75. | Bird | 76. | Fish |

| 77. Serpent | 78. Tree | 79. Plant | 80. Seed |
|---|---|---|---|
| 81. Shoe | 82. Crown | 83. Mantle | 84. Ball |
| 85. Talisman | 86. Mark | 87. Touchstone | 88. Colour |
| 89. Bowl | 90. Weapon | 91. Wand | 92. Crystal |
| 93. Word | 94. Dance | 95. Alphabet | 96. Number |
| 97. Moon | 98. Stars | 99. Sun | 100. Phases |
| 101. Time | 102. Edge | 103. Axis | 104. Centre |
| 105. Rim | 106. Tangent | 107. Transformation | 108. Betrayal |
| 109. Abandonment | 110. Salvation | 111. Body | 112. Blood |
| 113. Flesh | 114. Egg | 115. Essence | 116. Pact |
| 117. Promise | 118. Faith | 119. Doubt | 120. Mind |
| 121. Dream | 122. Feeling | 123. Game | 124. Goal |
| 125. Journey | 126. Destination | 127. Puzzle | 128. Growth |
| 129. Healing | 130. Help | 131. Opposites | 132. Action |
| 133. Stillness | 134. Identity | 135. Imagination | 136. Inner/Outer |
| 137. Ladder | 138. Hierarchy | 139. Retrospection | 140. Memory |
| 141. Forgetfulness | 142. Mirror | 143. Origin | 144. Ritual |
| 145. Split | 146. Wholeness | 147. Theft | 148. Union |
| 149. Unknown | 150. Wheel | 151. Web | 152. Age |

To allow children to use the selection of motifs, either give each child a copy of Table 5.2 or create an A3 poster or larger. Also, write the numbers 1–152 on separate scraps of paper or card and put these in an envelope so that motifs can be chosen at random.

Some ideas for using motifs:

- Select a motif and ask children to think of as many contexts for it as possible. So 'plant' would include a living thing that is not an animal, a place where manufacturing takes place, to set something in a particular position. Extend the activity by asking children to come up with sentences illustrating these contexts.

- Select a motif and create an association web. Essentially this is a brainstorming activity where all the ideas children come up with are included.

- Choose two motifs at random and think of as many links between them as possible. I just drew '19. companion' and '84. ball' out of the envelope, so:

> I went to the ball with my companion.
>
> My football is like a constant companion.
>
> A *Companion to the ballroom* is a book about dancing.
>
> The word companion has two 'o's in it and the letter 'o' is shaped like a ball.

- Use the motifs as a planning device for creative writing. The mind has a natural propensity to make connections, so children will tend to create a narrative 'organically' either by casting their eyes casually over the list, or by choosing motifs at random and noticing the stream of thoughts passing through the mind. (Interestingly, the word narrative derives from the Latin *narratus*, 'to come to know'.) It is not uncommon, when in a creative mood, for writers to find themselves taken by surprise as an idea pops into mind unbidden: in other words it has not been forced, although the groundwork has been done to prompt the flow of thoughts.

This technique is most effective if children have already made a few basic decisions. Ideally, they should have a theme or themes for the story, poem or whatever. A theme is an underpinning idea that binds the elements of the story together. Several of the items in the list could serve as themes; trial, threshold, life/death, bond, transformation, betrayal, abandonment, promise, memory and theft. Themes in themselves are often quite vague and generalised concepts, with individual pieces of writing being ways of exploring them in particular contexts.

It's also helpful at this stage if young writers know what genre they want to work in. The theme of betrayal could be written as a fantasy story, science fiction, crime thriller etc.

So let's say a child has decided to write a fantasy story with the theme of betrayal. Casting our eyes over the list, in a state of 'relaxed alertness', simply noticing thoughts coming to mind, the following ideas might surface:

> An adventurer meets a wise guide along the way.

> The king has been betrayed by his official enchanter.

> He has bound her with spells and demands something to release her.

> The wise guide tells of a magic blade that can cut the binding spells, but needs the adventurer's help to find it.

> The adventurer becomes the wise guide's companion.

> Their first trial during their quest is to come upon a mirror that always reflects the truth.

> They each learn something about themselves that surprises them (not sure what yet).

> Further trials involve the basic elements of earth, air, fire and water . . .

And so on. Note that it's fine for children at this stage of their thinking not to know all the answers yet. There is still a degree of vagueness to the ideas above, though these are likely to become clearer and more detailed as planning continues.

A further useful tool is to pause from time to time to review the ideas that have come along and ask some questions about them:

> What does the adventurer look like?

> Why is he or she seeking adventures?

> Why might the enchanter have betrayed the king? What does the enchanter want?

How does the wise guide know of the magic blade?

Why does the wise guide need help to find the blade?

It's not vital that these questions should be answered immediately. As the creative flow continues one or more possible answers might well come to mind as children cast their eyes over the list of motifs.

Emphasise to the children too that it's fine for them to change their minds and make their own decisions. So maybe it's a prince that has been bound by spells rather than a princess, or maybe the wise guide seems like a 'good guy' to begin with, but is actually the enchanter who deceives the adventurer into helping him to possess the blade before the king and his soldiers can find it. (And that idea just popped into mind, prompting me to think 'I didn't know I knew that until then!')

The grid can also be used analytically when looking at other people's creative writing as children 'tease out' themes and motifs of stories they read, or that you read with them.

## URBAN LEGENDS

Urban legends form a subgenre of the folk tale. They are often bizarre, funny and sometimes gruesome stories which are alleged to be true. Part of their seductiveness and persuasive power stems from the use of seemingly precise details of place, time and characters involved.

A typical urban legend tells of an elderly lady called Lena Beech who still lives at Number 42 West Street in a nearby town. Since her husband Ben died some years ago her only company has been a little poodle called Trixie. Well, the friend of a friend of mine – who is a near neighbour of Mrs Beech – heard that not long ago she went shopping on a Monday as she usually does and of course took Trixie with her. Mrs Beech's habit was to walk to the supermarket and catch a bus back.

On this particular day Mrs Beech was delayed longer than usual at the checkout and missed her bus by a minute. Since another wasn't due for the best part of an hour, she walked home with Trixie in tow. On the way back it started to rain and the poor dog was soaked and shivering by the time they reached Mrs Beech's front door. Panicking lest Trixie should develop a cold or pneumonia, Mrs Beech did what first occurred to her to dry the dog off quickly, and put Trixie in the microwave because she'd heard that works quickly. It was a Kenwood microwave and one of the last things her late husband had ever bought for her . . .

There are many collections of urban folk tales or 'Friend Of A Friend' ('FOAF') tales. Some that I recommend are listed below. The value of using them is that:

- Most of the stories are brief and very intriguing. They are a vehicle for teaching listening skills and can help extend children's concentration spans.
- Children see examples of concise, convincing narratives modelling many techniques they can incorporate in their own work.
- Many urban folk tales have a large number of variations. Children see how changing a few details can change the story radically. They also gain experience of the idea of 'variations on a theme'.
- Many urban legends display the qualities of parables and illustrate how stories can be 'templates' for conveying values and strategies for behaviour. In this sense urban folk tales amount to cultural symbols.
- Deeper study of urban legends opens up discussion of what is truth, distinctions between fact and fiction, how we arrive at our beliefs and how language can be used to influence and manipulate.

As well as simply reading such stories to the children, you might consider using them like this:

- Look at the different categories of story ranging from so-called 'earthy tales' and gossip (which include some urban legends) through family and history tales, to 'wonder tales', legends and myths. In traditional storytelling this 'hierarchy' of story types is called the 'Ladder to the Moon'. (For more details, see Bowkett, S., Harding, T., Lee, T. and Leighton, R. *Success in the Creative Classroom*, London: Network Continuum, 2007.)

- Tease out the themes of urban folk tales and have children write their own legends using these themes.
- Explore variations of selected legends and help the children to make up more.
- Use urban folk tales to develop children's storytelling skills. The books of American folklorist Jan Harold Brunvand are among the best. I recommend:

*The Vanishing Hitchiker: American Urban Legends and Their Meanings*, London: Picador, 1983.

*Curses! Broiled Again!*, New York: Norton, 1990.

*The Baby Train and Other Lusty Urban Legends*, New York: Norton, 1993.

You might also try:

Goss, M. *The Evidence for Phantom Hitch-Hikers*, Wellingborough, Northamptonshire: Aquarian Press, 1984.
Smith, P. *The Book of Nasty Legends*, Glasgow: Fontana/Collins, 1984.

Note that some of the subject matter in these books is perhaps not suitable for the age range of children in the Jumpstart! series. Use your own discretion in choosing the stories.

## RANDOM POEM

A popular novelty gift these days is magnetic fridge poetry. This is a boxful of words with magnetic backs. The words can be stuck to a fridge to make up poems. The same game can be played by writing words on scraps of paper, which the children then arrange into a suitable form. Here are a few variations of the basic idea:

## Mind the gap

Create random poems based on a given sentence structure. 'The ____ ____ on the ____', for instance. More complex structures can be suggested for children with a more sophisticated knowledge of grammar: 'The adjective or adjectival clause/noun or pronoun/verb or verb phrase/adverbial clause/preposition the adjective/noun.'

## Random haiku

Haiku are usually defined as brief three-line poems with a syllabic pattern of five-seven-five. I have to confess that they are among my very favourite kinds of poetry. When I run a haiku workshop with children I point out that many of the poems attempt to open the reader's eyes and heart to the wonder and the beauty of the world, sometimes by counterpointing a small vivid detail with the wider context. A simple 'template' for practising this way of seeing is to draw a triangle. At the top place the detail, at the left corner place the general context and at the right corner place an insight (sometimes in the form of another detail). See Figure 5.2 on page 124 for examples.

One useful way of randomising the haiku is to have the children practise creating them to the template suggested above with each line written on a scrap of paper. Alternatively, copy the lines of published haiku onto scraps for the children to use. Mixing and matching lines can sometimes produce beautiful and quite profound images.

A variation of the activity is to make 'urban haiku'. These use the cityscapes that many children know and endeavour to shift the reader's (and writer's) perspective to see them in a fresh way:

Burned out car. Wasteland

willowherb blooms anyway

October morning.

Grey factory smoke

my eyes follow upwards. Look!

Starlings still gather!

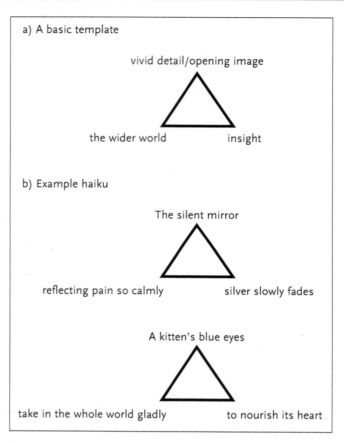

a) A basic template

vivid detail/opening image

the wider world          insight

b) Example haiku

The silent mirror

reflecting pain so calmly          silver slowly fades

A kitten's blue eyes

take in the whole world gladly          to nourish its heart

**Figure 5.2:** Haiku poems

## Consequences

Interesting and often amusing semi-narrative poems can arise out of using a 'Consequences' template, such as the one below. Ask the children to write a short response to each question or statement on pieces of paper. Collect the responses and put each 'category' into a separate envelope. Each child then randomly selects a scrap from every envelope and arranges them in the right order.

- Name a place.
- What is the weather like?
- Something interesting is happening not far away – what is it?
- Character A is walking along. What is his/her name?
- What is (s)he saying?
- Character A is carrying an unusual object. What is it?
- Character A meets Character B. What does A say?
- What does B say?
- What does B do?
- What does A say in reply?
- What does A do?
- What happens now?
- Think of a funny last line.

### 'Love is . . .'

For this game you will need a box or other suitable container filled with bits and pieces from the classroom or from around the house. Tell the children they are going to make a poem called 'Love is . . .' (or whatever theme you wish – feelings work well, as do themes such as 'the last day of term', 'homework', etc.). Give a few examples of the kinds of things you want the children to write:

- Love is a stone, solid and unchanging.
- Love is a whiteboard marker pen that can't stop scrawling 'I love you'.
- Love is the great book I'm reading. I would hate it to end.

Point out that the emotional tone of the responses can be serious or funny (but not inappropriate or insulting). Either pick items one at a time out of the box yourself, or invite the children to do it. Emphasise that it doesn't matter if an item fails to suggest an idea: if an idea comes along, that's fine, but don't struggle or try to force the words.

When around ten items have been drawn from the box, ask the children to discard any responses that they're not pleased with. Then have two big envelopes ready, one for serious responses and one for funny responses. Collect the children's work in the appropriate envelopes.

The children can now work individually, in pairs or in small groups. Each picks out some responses from one of the envelopes and creates a poem by shuffling the pieces of paper, modifying the ideas as necessary.

## WORD PYRAMID

Draw a triangle and mark it out as in Figure 5.3. Children can use this template as a way of building their vocabulary.

My own opinion is that wordplay increases children's passive vocabularies (the words they know and understand) and lifts more of those words into their active vocabularies (the words they actually use).

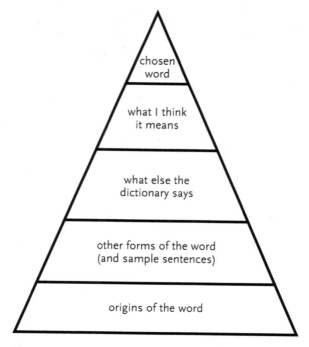

**Figure 5.3:** Word pyramid

This process is accelerated, I believe, when we as teachers model the attitude that we all own language equally, that words belong to us, and that being able to communicate effectively is both personally satisfying and a powerful social skill. If we as adults enjoy words, the chances are increased that our children will too. We can also usefully suggest (implicitly or overtly) that what counts is our endeavour to find the words that say what's in our heads, and not to get too hung up on technical accuracy during this essentially creative stage. Specific strategies for boosting children's confidence in language use include:

- Realising that 'mistakes' children make often reveal an *emergent understanding* of how the language is used. So instead of simply correcting the child who says 'Yesterday I wented to the shops with my mum', we can recognise that the child is developing an understanding of the past tense and already knows that 'ed' endings on verbs sometimes convey that tense. I think that children learn to use language more effectively when we model appropriate usage (I am reluctant to say 'correct usage') rather than simply correcting errors.
- Crediting children for using vivid and evocative language (foul language excepted!). Creativity is sometimes defined as 'going beyond the given'. When a child comes up with an unconventional/original use of language I usually offer sincere praise. For example, recently in a writing workshop a child described the sky as being 'not really dark, but it's got a hint of dark'. I immediately gave him a merit point for the vividness and descriptive power of that phrase 'a hint of dark', and I suggested it would make a great title for a story (I also told him to use it before I beat him to it!).
- Raising children's awareness of the effects that words have on them. Some time ago a little girl talked about the 'yellowish autumn leaves'. I told her that was a clever use of language and I asked the rest of the children what they imagined when they heard that phrase. Some children used entire sentences to describe the colours and shades of leaves that were evoked by that one word 'yellowish'. I pointed out that putting an 'ish' or 'ee' sound on the end of colour-words usually makes the

listeners' imaginations do a lot of work. Most children also talked about memories and other associations with the word 'autumn'. 'So there you are,' I told that little girl, 'just look at all the things your phrase has accomplished!' She was very pleased, though we were inundated with 'ish' and 'ee' colour-words for the rest of the session . . .

- Understanding that as teachers one of the most powerful things we can say to children is 'I don't know – but how might we find out?'

Use the word pyramid technique as a way of allowing children to investigate new vocabulary in stories and other texts they study. Here are a few more ideas:

- Word of the day. Pick an interesting word and give the children some time to investigate it further, perhaps using the word pyramid template.
- Word mobiles. Help the children to make mobiles tracing how root words are used.
- 'Yes, but not in the South'. The writer Stephen Potter (1900–1969) is perhaps best known for inventing the idea of 'one-upmanship' – getting ahead in life by being 'one up' on your rivals. He developed his ideas in books such as *Some Notes on Lifemanship, The Theory and Practice of Gamesmanship, Supermanship* and others. The excellent film comedy *School for Scoundrels* (1959) tells the story of how a social failure (played by Ian Carmichael) enrols in the College of Lifemanship under Alastair Sim's tutelage to become one up in his dealings with other people.

One of Stephen Potter's one-upmanship tricks is to take a vague but reasonable-sounding phrase and drop it into conversation at a strategic point. If said with conviction it gives the speaker an air of authority and even charisma as being 'someone who knows what (s)he's talking about'. One of my own favourites is 'Yes, but not in the South'. You can turn this into a wordplay game by having the children invent and search for such phrases, which they can then use in an appropriate context.

*Tip*: Try out this technique yourself first, at a staff meeting, perhaps. Here are a few phrases you might consider using:

- Of course only if the trend continues upward.
- The Classics are full of it.
- Especially during the Middle Ages.
- Which clearly indicates an up-down divide.
- Most usually around the ankles.

## SPOT THE DIFFERENCE

This simple game invites children to discuss differences between similar words. For instance, how do we distinguish between:

- Big, large, colossal
- Jealousy, envy, spite
- Run, hurry, rush
- Beautiful, gorgeous, attractive?

Playing this game encourages children to develop their sensibilities as they strive towards the subtle differences in meaning between words.

## SEMIOPATHY

This term was apparently coined in *New Scientist* magazine a few years ago. It refers to a sign or notice whose intended meaning can be interpreted in other ways. 'This window is alarmed' is an obvious example (and tempts the rejoinder 'And the door was pretty shocked too!'). Other examples are:

- Dogs Must Be Carried on the Escalators (but I don't have a dog!).
- Slow Children Crossing (quick ones mustn't cross).
- Heavy Plant Turning (look at the size of that cactus!).
- Watch Batteries Fitted (but you don't have to look if you don't want to).

- Fire Exit (the fire can't exit anywhere else?).
- Parking Fine (well personally I had some difficulty).

Here are some to work out for yourself before trying them out on the children:

- Extra Thick Baby Wipes.
- Police Club Visitors.
- Attract Men With Bushy Beards.
- Protective Goggles Must Be Worn.
- Crocodiles Do Not Swim Here.

## JOKES

The benefits of humour and laughter in education are now well known (see, for example, Smith, A. *The Brain's Behind It*, London: Network Educational Press, 2002). Extensive research indicates that laughing lowers blood pressure, reduces stress hormones, increases muscle flexion and boosts immune function by raising levels of infection-fighting T-cells, disease-fighting proteins called interferon gamma and B-cells, which produce disease-destroying antibodies. Laughter also triggers the release of endorphins, the body's natural painkillers, and produces a general feeling of well-being (I laughed out loud when my doctor told me that).

There is no doubt that learning ability is inhibited in environments of low creative/intellectual challenge and high stress, whereas learning flourishes where there is low stress, often engendered by humour, combined with increasing challenge and diversity of tasks. The 'laughter factor' also engages and sustains concentration and interest, while a sense of levity helps children to feel comfortable in the presence of ambiguity and uncertainty in their learning – in other words, to feel comfortable not knowing the right answer right now, but being prepared to investigate further. Finally, and not least, the understanding of jokes is a creative act where unexpected connections are realised. Many jokes are *reframes*, sudden experiences of looking at something in a different way. Appreciating and constructing jokes rehearses those two vital elements of creativity:

- Making new mental links.
- Looking at things in different ways.

Here are a few school jokes to demonstrate the point:

- A little girl had just finished her first week of school. 'I'm wasting my time,' she said to her mother. 'I can't read, I can't write – and now they won't let me talk!'
- The Chairman of Governors was being shown around the school. His tour included a Y6 Maths lesson. He took time to look at every child's book and say something encouraging to each pupil. Coming up to Harry's table he saw that the young lad had already finished the exercise. 'That's good work Harry,' the Chairman of Governors said, smiling. 'You're obviously very able at Maths. What do you want to be when you grow up?' 'An accountant sir,' said Harry. 'Really? You need to be extremely good to be one of those. So tell me what does 983 plus 437 make?' Harry grinned and winked. 'What would you like it to make?' he replied.
- Another Maths joke:

  *Teacher*: Chloe, what is sixteen plus sixteen?
  *Chloe*: Thirty-two sir.
  *Teacher*: Hmm that's pretty good.
  *Chloe*: Pretty good – it's perfect!

- How did the Vikings send messages to each other? By Norse Code.
- What do you get if you cross a vampire with the National Curriculum? Lots of blood tests.
- Where was the American Declaration of Independence signed? At the bottom.

A few more humorous scenarios:

  *Teacher*: Tyler, why haven't you got your homework book for me this morning?
  *Tyler*: Miss, I lost it fighting a kid who said you weren't the best teacher in the entire world.

*Teacher*: Now then class, whatever question I ask you I want you all to answer at once. What is sixteen plus sixteen?
*Class*: At once!

*Teacher*: Now class, I am happy to say that we will have only half a day of school this morning.
*Class*: Hooray!
*Teacher*: And we'll have the other half day of school this afternoon.

*Son*: I can't go to school today Dad. I don't feel well.
*Father*: Where don't you feel well?
*Son*: In school.

*Teacher* (to new pupil): Are you any good at English, Susie?
*Susie*: Yes and no.
*Teacher*: What does that mean?
*Susie*: Yes I'm no good at English.

*Teacher* (taking the register): Connor, you missed school yesterday, didn't you?
*Connor*: Not very much.

Finally, six rules to improve your writing:

1. Avoid alliteration. Always.
2. Never use a long word when a diminutive one will do.
3. Be more or less specific.
4. Do not put statements in the negative.
5. And don't start a sentence with a conjunction. Remember too, a preposition is a terrible word to end a sentence with.
6. Read through your work carefully to see if you have any words out.

Exploit the educational value of jokes in these ways:

- Build humour into your teaching (if it isn't there already!). Remember the many benefits of laughter.
- Use humorous similes to create vivid impressions in the ideas you offer. A joke my A Level Biology teacher made (many moons ago) was that 'Sea anemones stuck to the rocks after the tide has gone out look like half-sucked wine gums.' It makes me smile even now, and furthermore I will never forget that comparison.

- Explore double- or multi-meanings of words in jokes. Use this as a way of heightening the children's awareness of ambiguity in language.
- Explore the structure of humour and the patterns that many jokes rely on. For instance, the *pattern of three* is common. This is also a rhetorical device much used in the language of persuasion.
- Study the methods of stand-up comedians. Use these as appropriate to develop children's presentational skills, communication skills generally and self-confidence.
- Use wacky and fantastical premises as (jump)starting points for some of the creativity games in this book. This immediately creates a safe environment where the children aren't worrying about 'real' facts and right answers. Nevertheless, the thinking they do and the insights they have can usually be applied to the curriculum and the real world.

## PLAYING WITH PROVERBS

The nuggets of wisdom we call proverbs have been around for thousands of years and exist in all cultures. Many of them are pertinent and useful to us today, so for that reason alone they are worth studying.

However, they can also be used to help develop children's thinking and creative wordplay.

- Create a selection of proverbs. Discuss their meanings with the children, who then have to bring them up to date. So, for example:
  - Original proverb: 'A bird in the hand is worth two in the bush'. This means: It is better to have something actually in your possession than two things (or twice as much) that are not. Space-age versions: 'An smartphone in my pocket is worth two in the shop' or 'A fact in my head is worth two in a book I never open.'

○ Some examples may seem to go against the agreed definition. So: 'A rocket in orbit is worth two on the launch pad'.
In this case the rocket is 'worth' more because it's fulfilling
its purpose, while the rockets still sitting on the launch pad
are not. Exploring variations like this helps children to understand the deeper meaning of proverbs.

*Tip*: Many proverbs lend themselves to philosophical discussion. In this case the word 'worth' is worth exploring. What do
the children think the word means? Look at related words like
'worthy' and 'worthless'. What do they mean? How do we use
them? Is the 'worth' of a smartphone the same as the 'worth'
of a fact that you know? (This leads on to thinking about cost
and value.)

- Look for two or more proverbs that sum up a similar idea:
  'You've put the cart before the horse'/'You've closed the stable
  door after the horse has bolted'.
- Find two proverbs that contradict one another (or make up a
  proverb that says the opposite of one you've found): 'Those who
  make best use of their time have none to spare'/'Those who use
  their hours wisely always have time in hand'.
- Explore the idea that many proverbs express a point of view
  or an opinion, rather than a fact. 'A heavy purse makes a light
  heart'. Work with the children to think of examples where this
  might not be true. Suppose a very rich man had just lost a close
  friend to an illness. No amount of money could have saved her.
  Would a heavy purse still make a light heart then?
- Highlight the idea that many proverbs are metaphors. Help
  children to understand that such proverbs stand for something
  else. 'Wash your dirty linen at home'. This can be literally true
  (unless you use a launderette) but generally means 'keep personal matters and indiscretions in the family'.
- Bearing the metaphorical nature of proverbs in mind, create
  new ones using myths and legends: 'Wherever there is treasure,
  you'll find a dragon' or 'Lightning never strikes twice – unless
  the god of thunder decides otherwise'.

- Summarise fables and fairy tales in a proverb: 'Grapes out of reach will always be sour' or 'Leaving the straight and narrow path will lead you to the wolf's jaws'.
- Create proverbs based on topics you are studying. So if, for example, you are studying countries and landforms, suitable proverbs might be:
  - The boundaries of a country are drawn in people's minds.
  - Migrating birds are never troubled by a nation's name.
  - Fell one tree and make a fire. Fell a million trees and make a disaster.
  - Fallen rain is never lost – the clouds take it back to give rain again.

- Use proverbs to reflect your/the school's ethos of learning. Remember the metaphorical nature of some proverbs. Have the children create posters for display:
  - Opportunity is finer than gold.
  - Time lost can never be called back.
  - Nothing costs so much as what is given to us.
  - Give a man a fish and you feed him for a day. Teach a man to fish and you feed him for a lifetime. (Or as a fishing-fanatic friend of mine says: 'Teach a man to fish and you'll never see him at the weekend.')
  - Chopping your own firewood warms you twice.
  - A proverb is only as good as the one who uses it.

## NEW WORDS AND WORD COMBOS

We have already explored the idea that language is fluid and ever-changing. New words are added to the dictionary every year, while other terms fall out of use. Some areas of knowledge, such as computer technology, are developing so quickly that they feed huge numbers of new words into both the popular and the technical areas of language. Studying and inventing new terms is a great way of developing children's creativity through wordplay.

- Research new words and phrases. How did these terms come about? What do they mean? How are they appropriate? For example: smartphone, Bluetooth, Blackberry, iPod nano, blog, satnav . . .
- Prepare a list of prefixes and attach them to the names of everyday objects. What new gadgets come to mind? For example:
  - Anti (against) as in antigravity – anti-junkmail letterbox, anti-steam glass, anti-cold caller telephone.
  - Auto (self) as in autobiography – autoshower, autobed, autobook.
  - Meta (beyond) as in metamorphosis – metahome, metamobile, metapet, metapod nano.
- Invite the children to make up new collective nouns. Look at some unusual examples that already exist before brainstorming. So we already have a building of rooks, a muster of peacocks, a clowder of cats, a carillon of bells:
  - What new collective nouns might we attach to people talking together on their mobile phones/fallen leaves/homework books/children who've just come in muddied-up from play/shoppers queuing two days early for the January sales/people who all own a pink iPod nano?
  - What groups might these new collective nouns refer to: an apathy/a zing/a pointedness/a skiffle/an attainment/an illusion?
- Play the game of 'If you crossed A with B, you'd get . . . ?' Some years ago geneticists cross-bred a lion and a tiger and produced a liger (I don't know if they also made a tigon). There exists a tea company called Imporient. I think this word is a clever invention because it suggests 'imported from the Orient' and also 'imperial and important'. The word has grace and dignity as well as great descriptive power.

*Tip*: Add a kinaesthetic element to the game by printing out the words on card. Cut the words in two so that, for instance, giraffe becomes 'gi' and 'raffe' on separate cards. The children can then physically shift word fragments around to sift quickly through many combinations. Use themes or topics such as animals, machines or the names of food products. Younger children may prefer to work with pictures of animals, people in different occupations, etc. Another version of the game uses pictures of different superheroes taken from comics. Cut out and paste logos, weapons and gadgets from different characters to create a new super hero/heroine.

## MAKING NEW METAPHORS

Our language is metaphorical (representational) at two levels. Words themselves are not the things they refer to – the menu is not the meal and the map is not the land itself. And on a smaller scale we use endless metaphorical phrases as part of our day-to-day communication. Try looking at the following sayings *literally* for a moment, to see how far we take metaphor for granted:

- I'll give you a bell later today.
- I'm feeling under the weather.
- The run-up to Christmas.
- I'm all fingers and thumbs.
- (And my all-time favourite, from an unknown novel of yester-year . . . ) Her eyes twinkled, fluttered, met his, dropped to the floor then went back to the jewels. He picked them up, held them for a moment then returned them to her with a smile.

Metaphors are usually studied simply as one of the figures of speech and children are rightly encouraged to use effective and appropriate metaphors in their writing. One way of helping to ensure this is to raise awareness of the pervasiveness of metaphor through wordplay. Try out these activities with your class:

- Look at language with a literal eye. The short list of metaphors above makes the point. Encourage children to notice metaphorical expressions in people's everyday (or common or garden) language and to think up explanations of how those metaphors came about.

*Tip*: It's always worth researching the origins of the phrases and sayings we use, but give children the opportunity to make up their own explanations first.

For instance, what stories can the children make up to explain the origins of these expressions?

1. A red herring.
2. Dog days (roughly the six-week period from the start of July through to mid-August).
3. Honeymoon.
4. Being 'on tenterhooks' (to be anxious).
5. I've got a frog in my throat.

And the supposed explanations are:

1. Originally a red herring was literally a dried, smoked fish. It had a strong flavour and apparently if dragged across the path a fox had taken would draw the hounds off the fox's scent. Today the term refers to a spurious argument or a false clue or trail in a crime story.
2. The Romans believed that the influence of the star Sirius – also called the Dog Star, and the brightest star in the sky – made this period the hottest time of the year.
3. The word honeymoon comes from the old Germanic custom of drinking diluted honey for thirty days following a wedding feast (although the *Concise Oxford Dictionary* informs us that the term refers to a sixteenth-century expression meaning waning affection and not to a period of a month [the word 'month' deriving from moon – think 'moonth']).
4. A tenterground was an area where freshly prepared cloth was stretched out on tenterhooks to dry. The term comes from the Latin *tendere* meaning to stretch and is also the origin of tent – a portable shelter of stretched cloth.
5. To have a frog in one's throat means to have a 'croaky' voice. Originally the expression may have referred to (perhaps apocryphal) stories of people drinking from streams or wells and literally swallowing frogspawn. According to folk tradition the eggs would hatch in the victim and the frogs would have to be lured out (how, I wonder!) or the victim died a gruesome death.

*Source*: Radford, E. *To Coin A Phrase*, London: Arrow Books, 1974.

- Change the metaphors you notice. Here are a few that come immediately to mind:
  - I'm over the weather.
  - His alibi was below board.
  - They had their fronts to the wall.
  - She was the orange of her mother's eye.

- Make up new similes. Take a simile such as 'My tongue feels as rough as the bottom of a parrot's cage' and have the children brainstorm alternatives.
- Try ringing the changes on well-known rhyming similes. 'He was as snug as a bug in a rug' might become:
  - As snug as a cat in a flat.
  - As snug as a mouse in a house.
  - As snug as ten crows in a row.
  - As happy as a bear at the fair.
  - As fed-up as a fish in a dish.
  - As lost as a bee out to sea.

*Tip*: Make the game more kinaesthetic by preparing two sets of cards, one of adjectives ('snug', 'happy', 'lost', etc.) and one of animals and people. Encourage the children to pair up cards as inspiration for new similes.

## THE FLINTY WIND – MULTISENSORY METAPHORS

Because of the way the brain is 'wired up' we often cross-match sensory impressions when describing things (see also 'What colour is this music?' on page 40). We have already explored the way we describe feelings as colours. Very early on in their development children come to know the link between feelings and colours.

- Put up a colour chart – a visual display of different colours, such as the colour paint charts you find in DIY stores. Ask children to point out some of the colours and the feelings they are associated with. Take some of the colours that are left and ask children to suggest feelings that might match up with them. Do it the other way round, too. Say 'If surprise was a colour, what colour would it be?'

*Tip 1*: You may find that children who tend to think more visually will respond to this first. You can satisfy the more auditory thinkers in the class by matching feelings to musical instruments and other sounds. Tinkle a triangle, for instance, and say 'If this sound was a feeling, which one would it be?' Similarly, more kinaesthetic children might be more easily able to match textures with feelings.

The title of this section features a phrase used by the poet Dylan Thomas in a short story he wrote called *The Followers*, which is well worth reading for its powerful language and evocative atmosphere. Ask the children 'What would a flinty wind feel like on your skin?'

*Tip 2*: First impressions are likely to be truly synaesthetic. Some children take more time and think cognitively, i.e. they try and work out an answer without *experiencing* the effects of the phrase emotionally and in terms of physical sensation.

- Take the idea of a 'flinty' wind and encourage the children to create new metaphors using the same pattern. What would the following *feel* like?

  o A feathery wind.
  o A silky wind.
  o A candyfloss wind.
  o A waterfall wind.
  o A glassy wind.

- Extend the activity to sounds:

  o A snaredrum wind.
  o A tambourine wind.
  o A bassoon wind.
  o A mandolin wind (Rod Stewart fans will recognise this one).
  o A penny-whistle wind.

- Try it with colours too:

  o A silvery wind.
  o An aquamarine wind.
  o A bronzy wind.
  o A blue-white wind.
  o A maroon wind.

## THE ACRONYM GAME

An acronym is a word formed from the initial letters of other words. The word acronym derives from the Greek *akros*, 'topmost' (or 'first' [letter]) and *onoma*, 'name'. Some acronyms come to be treated as words in themselves and their origins are lost to many people. One example is 'laser', standing originally for Light Amplification by Stimulated Emission of Radiation. Another is 'radar', meaning RAdio Detection And Ranging.

Acronyms can serve as useful 'hooks' for the memory. Creating new acronyms encourages children to explore the ideas behind the word in more detail and can give rise to greater understanding.

- Help children make up new acronyms for feelings:

  o AWE – Amazing, Wonderful, Exciting!
  o LOVE – Lost in Others, Very Enjoyable.
  o ANGER – Allowing Niggles to Gnaw, Empathy Rejected.

- Invite the children to make acronyms out of their names:

  o Smiling Temperament, Energetic (can be) Vexing, Enthusiast.
  o Enjoys Doughnuts, Wild, Athletic, Reads Daily.
  o Shy, Argues Reasonably, Advises Honestly.

- Create acronyms that sum up important qualities. ADVENTURER – Always Determined, Very Energetic, Never Tires, Ultra-Restless, Ever-Roving.
- Try 'acronym poems' as a way of encouraging brevity and vividness in descriptive writing:

  o STAR – Shiny Tintack Alive with Radiance.
  o BEE – Buzzing Energetic Explorer.
  o SHEEP – Shaggy Heap Enduring, Endless Patience.

## WORDPLAY CARD GAMES

- Prepare a deck of cards featuring a list of words and their synonyms. *Roget's Thesaurus* is a good source for these. Shuffle and deal the deck to a group of three or four children, who hold their cards face down, unseen. Each child takes a turn in placing a card face up on the table. When a synonym is placed on the last card laid down the first child to shout 'Snap!' wins the pile.

- Matching Pairs. Place a number of synonym/antonym pairs of words face down on the table, randomly arranged. Each child has a go in turning up one card so that everyone in the group sees it, then replacing it face down. When a child spots a synonym/antonym pair, when it is his turn he can turn up both cards and, if he's correct, he wins the pair.

- Category Threes. Select a number of categories. These might be mammals, units of volume, units of time, capital cities, the names of mountains, etc. Create a deck of cards featuring three examples from each category. Tell the children who are playing that there is this number of cards for each of the categories you've selected. The game is then played like Matching Pairs: cards are turned up randomly and replaced face down. When a child has recognised all three cards in a given category, when it is his turn he turns all three face up and, if he's correct, wins all of those cards. Make the game more challenging by increasing the number of examples in each category.

- Gradations. Create a deck of cards made of graded lists. So, for example: hut, cottage, house, mansion, palace are graded in terms of size and grandeur; whispered, talked, shouted, roared and screamed are graded in terms of loudness. Do not always use the same number of words in each graded list. So, for example, one graded list might contain only four words, another list seven, etc. Make this fact clear to the children.

Shuffle and deal the whole deck among a group of four children. Also give each child one counter, each of a different colour. The children are allowed to look at their own hand of cards. The first child places one of his cards face up on the table. If the next child has an 'upgrade' card ('shouted' to put on top of 'whispered', for instance) she can play her card and put her counter beside the pile to indicate that she's in the lead at the moment. However, she might choose not to play the card if it is at the top of the category – if she has 'screamed', she can wait until all other cards in that category have been laid down. She can then top the lot with her card and win the pile.

If a child does not have a card to place on the category pile that has been started, he can begin another category beside it. The fun of the game is in wondering if any of the other players have a category card to beat your best.

- Parts and Wholes. Create a set of category cards, e.g. mammal, bird, fish, etc. and a set of 'parts' cards, any of which may apply to one or more of the categories: has wings, can swim, is warm-blooded, lays eggs, etc.

Lay out the selection of category cards face up on the table, then shuffle and deal the parts cards. The children can look at their own hand of parts cards. The first child to play lays down one parts card, e.g. has wings. If the next child has a parts card that can be added to the first card because they can both apply to the same category, e.g. lays eggs, then she can play that card. At this stage the parts cards might refer to birds or insects. The third child plays another parts card (if he has one) that will add to the category. If he wants to play safe, he can also select a category card, place it on top of the pile and win that pile for himself. However, he might choose not to do that if he thinks that he can win a bigger pile of parts cards at his next turn – though he runs the risk of another player winning the category with a smaller pile of parts cards in the meantime.

## SYNONYM/ANTONYM TREE

This can be created as a wall display or a word mobile can be fashioned using the same idea. Begin with a root word that has evolved into many variations, e.g. *manus*, meaning 'hand'. Place this among the roots of your tree and draw a trunk coming up out of the soil. The children's task is to create branches for the tree. Each branch points to a variation of the root word – manual, manufacture, manuscript, etc. Beside each variation is placed a single-word antonym or a phrase that sums up an opposite meaning – automated, grow, printed, etc. If you are making a mobile instead of a tree wall display, synonyms and antonyms can be written on either side of cards dangling from wire hangers.

You can extend the tree or mobile idea by using Gradations, Parts and Wholes, etc., as described above.

## SATNAV

This is a game to develop children's instructional language and map-reading skills. You will need some detailed maps – OS 1:50,000 Landranger Series is ideal. Children may work individually or in pairs and plan a route from A to B, referring to as many standard map symbols as possible and working in distances rather than mentioning place names. Ask the children to write in the second person (the 'you' voice). When this activity is done with older children, what they come up with might sound something like this:

> Start out from the centre of Uppingham town 86.7 99.9 (remembering the co-ordinates rule of 'along the corridor and up the stairs'). Travel south for approximately 8 kilometres. During this journey you will pass a reservoir to the West (your right), which may be visible from the road. Then you will come to a small village and reach a junction with a secondary road (marked in orange) which for a short way runs close alongside the tunnel of a dismantled railway. But do not take this road. Instead, continue along the road you have been travelling on. After a very short time you will see a turning to your right (if you pass the inn on your left, you have gone too far!). Take this minor road: it goes for about 2 kilometres and then forks at the centre of another village. Take the left-hand fork and soon you will pass a small school on your left . . .

The work of younger children will presumably be simpler, and you may in fact choose to work with less complicated maps. When each child or pair has completed the route, they swap with another group, who attempt to retrace the path.

*Tip 1*: Add interest by turning the game into a treasure hunt. Supply each group with a small gift or treat – sweets perhaps (or, more healthily, some fruit). If the recipient group finds the place where the treasure has been hidden, they win it for themselves.

*Tip 2*: Add a kinaesthetic element to the activity by using your school itself. Children hide their treasure and then plan a route, perhaps with riddles and puzzles included, for other groups to work out.

*Tip 3*: Many children enjoy drawing to accompany their writing. Encourage them to use standard map symbols and terms to create their own landscape, which can then be used as the setting for their stories. Also, see below for a variation of this idea.

## CHOOSE YOUR OWN ADVENTURE

Many children will be familiar with the *Fighting Fantasy* books that first appeared in the early 1980s and which are still popular today. The basic concept is that a story is created with many alternative routes through it. The reader/explorer encounters a situation and is presented with a choice of what to do. If he chooses option A, he is directed to one part of the book; if he chooses B, he must go to another part. Further decisions guide the reader through the tree-like narrative. Sometimes bad decisions lead to the loss of 'health points', weapons or treasure and can result in injury and even the death of the 'player-character', in which case the child must start again. I have known even very reluctant readers to persevere for a long time with books like these, determined to make the right decisions and survive to the end of the story.

Simple 'choose-your-own-adventure' tales can be created by children using maps as visual organisers for the planning of their work. To keep the activity involving from the start, I suggest you make the following preparations:

- Organise the children into small working groups of two or three. Each group invents a character for the story. For some tips on character creation, try Bowkett, S. *Boys and Writing*, London: Network Continuum Pocket PAL series, 2006. Apart from a brief physical description of the character, (s)he can be given certain traits such as strength, intelligence, speed, honesty, etc.

*Tip*: Some children, who collect trading cards based on TV series or comic-book heroes, will be very familiar with this idea and can explain things to you further. Rate each trait on a one-to-six scale. The traits may be chosen randomly by the roll of a dice, or children can decide for themselves on a rating. In this case, point out that characters are much more interesting if they have weaknesses as well as strengths. Note too that ratings may change during the course of the story based on the player-character's decisions.

- Work up a basic storyline. You might want all of the children to work with the same basic plot and genre. If different groups prefer to work within different genres, make the storyline very general: 'An evil ruler through his greed is bringing the land to ruin. A group of local people decide to try and overthrow him . . .', etc. When the plot is this generalised it can be developed as a fantasy story, a romance, a murder mystery and so on.
- Make it clear to the children that the setting of their story will be the landscape featured on the maps you supply. Children can adapt these to suit their purposes, but point out that using the map will help them to keep track of their adventures.
- Overlay each map with a large sheet of greaseproof paper or tracing paper of some sort. Children can then annotate the map without marking it directly. Alternatively, let them use Post-it notes on the map itself.
- Have the children discuss how the story begins. Most importantly, where are the player-characters located on the map (they do not need to be together)? And what gets the plot moving – a sudden crisis, danger or the wish to find treasure or defeat an enemy? What event prompts the characters to action?
- Each group now begins to move the character across the map. Groups of children may join forces and work from the same map sheet: their characters may travel together or meet each other along the way. You will need to guide the children so that the story remains exciting. Soon after the start of the narrative, the character must face a decision. It might be as simple as a road junction – does your character turn left or right (and why?) – or perhaps it's an encounter with another person or creature, or maybe the character finds something significant.

- Ask the children to write each decision point as a brief scene from the story in the second person. Each scene will require the character to make a choice. The chosen option forms the basis for the next scene. The option that was not chosen is still noted down, however, as this can supply ideas for later on in the story.
- The children of course are making up the narrative as they go along, working in puzzles and mysteries, exciting fight scenes, intriguing encounters or scary settings. They may not even be producing polished writing at this stage but simply hammering out a workable plot and making brief notes about what happens. Their annotations are written on the greaseproof paper overlay/ the Post-its as the characters progress across the map.

*Tip*: You can make the game more interesting for the children by adding material of your own for them to work with. Here are some ideas:

- Chance cards. Create a set of chance cards which will bring good or bad fortune to a character. The cards will feature ideas like 'Find a weapon. You can use this but once', 'You fall and injure yourself. Lose three health points', 'You learn something to your advantage – what will it be?' If children get stuck in their story, they can pick up a chance card and this might prompt further ideas in them.
- Encounters. Suggest that if two enemies meet, they can settle the encounter by each one rolling the dice. The higher score wins the encounter. You can use the flip of a coin to answer certain closed questions about the situation – use heads for yes and tails for no. The children can ask questions like 'Can my character still walk?' 'Will my character's wound become infected?' 'Can I take my opponent's weapons now?' This adds detail to the scene and provides ideas to continue with the narrative.
- Consider appointing a storymaster to oversee each group. This takes the pressure off you trying to guide every group simultaneously! The job of the storymaster will be to supply ideas, see that fair play is maintained, help to annotate the map and/or scribe the story and generally to assist the other children towards a completed storyline.

- When a group has finished an adventure they will have a sequence of events roughly worked out which brings a character to a point where the treasure has been found, the princess has been rescued, the villain has been captured, etc. This, if you like, is the 'successful' route through the adventure. The children should have a clear sense of setting for the tale and have accumulated some descriptive details.
- You might want each child now simply to refine and add detail to the storyline and to write it up as a straight piece of fiction. Another option is to get the groups to look back over the earlier options that were not chosen. If they had been, what would have happened? The children can now develop these other situations as alternative routes (which ultimately might still lead the character to a satisfactory resolution).
- Each completed adventure (the successful route plus some alternatives) becomes a resource for use with different classes. As these other children move a character across the map, following the guidance of the original story, have them add detail to the adventure, visualise and describe scenes in more detail, role-play different scenes, create dialogue which they can record, and so on.

*Tip*: Children might wish to create their own maps as the basis for a choose-your-own-adventure. This is fine, although printed maps do offer plenty of detail. Adventures can be based on stories the children already know, thus much of the work of character creation, detail of place and so on has already been done. Also, many fantasy novels actually feature maps, which children can use as a basis for further adventures in that world. Some stories that come to mind are *The Lord of the Rings*, *The Hobbit* (J.R.R. Tolkien), *The Weirdstone of Brisingamen*, *The Moon of Gomrath*, *Elidor* (Alan Garner), *Eragon* (Christopher Paolini), *The Doomspell Trilogy* (Cliff McNish), *Wolf Brother – Chronicles of Ancient Darkness* (Michelle Paver).